355.0217
TAY   Taylor, L. B.

           The nuclear arms race

THE NUCLEAR ARMS RACE

THE
NUCLEAR
ARMS
RACE

BY L. B. TAYLOR, JR.

FRANKLIN WATTS
NEW YORK/LONDON/TORONTO/SYDNEY/1982
AN IMPACT BOOK

Photographs courtesy of:
U.S. Navy Photos: pp. 28, 60;
U.S. Air Force Photos: pp. 4, 24, 25, 75;
Official Dept. of Defense Photo: p. 29;
United Press International: p. 64;
Sidney Harris: opp. title page, p. 81;
Renault (Rothco): p. 89;
Graham (Rothco): p. 95.

Library of Congress Cataloging in Publication Data

Taylor, L. B.
The nuclear arms race.

(An Impact book)
Bibliography: p. 97
Includes index.
Summary: Discusses how the present nuclear
arms buildup came about, compares the
military strengths of the United States and
the Soviet Union, and examines attempts to
control the uses of the destructive weapons.
1. Atomic warfare—Juvenile literature.
2. Strategic forces—United States—Juvenile
literature. 3. Strategic forces—Soviet Union—
Juvenile literature. 4. Strategic Arms Limitation
Talks—Juvenile literature. 5. Peace—Juvenile
literature. [1. Atomic warfare. 2. Atomic
weapons. 3. Arms control] I. Title.
UF767.T33   355'.0217   81-21855
ISBN 0-531-04401-7   AACR2

CONTENTS

TO MY COUSIN JANE

THE NUCLEAR ARMS RACE

1

ARMAGEDDON

"Furthermore," continues the president, "we not only are still the strongest nation on earth, but we will remain so, if Congress approves our defense budget for the coming year."

The audience erupts in applause. The president is addressing a national convention of the American Legion, a fraternal organization made up of military veterans, in a large hall in Washington, D.C., only a few blocks from the White House.

Suddenly, a dark-suited Secret Service agent moves swiftly across the stage and hands the president a note. The president reads it and turns pale. "Excuse me," he says and walks briskly off the stage and out of sight. A murmur stirs among the Legionnaires.

In a small room in back of the convention hall, the president picks up a special emergency telephone operated by a communications team that is constantly with him wherever he travels. The chairman of the Joint Chiefs of Staff is on the other end of the line.

"Mr. President," he says solemnly, "we have absolute confirmation that the Soviet Union has launched a full-scale nuclear missile attack on the United States."

Stunned, the president asks, "Are you certain there can be no mistake, or that it wasn't an accidental launching?"

"We are positive beyond all doubt. There is no mistake. Our satellites in orbit have detected a massive launching of Soviet intercontinental ballistic missiles. They are headed toward us. This has been confirmed by radar sites and other sources."

"How much time do we have before they hit?" the president asks.

"Fifteen to twenty minutes at the most."

The president orders a retaliatory missile attack on the Soviets. He instructs his press secretary to notify the television and radio networks so they can make an emergency announcement. Then he and his top aides depart for the White House, where Marine helicopters will take them to specially constructed nuclear bomb shelters built into a mountainside in nearby Virginia.

Daytime television and radio shows are interrupted, as sober-faced commentators broadcast the warning. People are told not to panic. They are advised to remain in their homes or office buildings or factories—not to go outside. But thousands panic anyway. They stream out of the buildings where they work in an effort to get home to their families. Streets become jammed with cars, and roads are quickly blocked.

"If you have a basement or cellar, stay there," the commentators announce. "If you don't have a basement, get under a table in the middle of a room, away from windows. Fill your bathtubs with drinking water."

In shopping centers and stores, people run out into the parking lots, screaming hysterically. Schoolchildren are assembled in auditoriums and libraries. Farmhands run through the fields to warn others of the impending danger. Tens of thousands of people in large cities and small towns hurry to churches to pray. Telephone lines quickly become hopelessly overloaded as people try to reach their loved ones.

The nation's military goes on immediate alert. At air bases

around the country, squadrons of missile-carrying B-52 bombers taxi to the ends of runways and take off in wave after wave.

In several western states, Minuteman and Titan intercontinental ballistic missiles in underground silos are put on alert and begin launch procedures. In the Atlantic, Pacific, and Indian oceans, dozens of submarines armed with nuclear missiles begin countdowns for launching their weapons at Soviet targets. In Western Europe, North Atlantic Treaty Organization (NATO) troops rush to their posts in anticipation of follow-up attacks by Soviet tactical and conventional military forces.

In cities and towns across the United States, church bells ring and fire alarms blare constantly to warn those who have not yet heard the news. On the highways, word is passed by CB radio. Still, millions will not get the word in time.

Less than twenty minutes from the initial warning signal, the first wave of nuclear warheads strikes. With alarming accuracy, they land on their targets—U.S. missile bases in western states. Each individual warhead creates a blast more than several hundred times the strength of the atomic bombs that were dropped in 1945 on the Japanese cities of Hiroshima and Nagasaki.

Each blast sends out a gigantic concussive force that smashes all buildings above ground for miles around, instantly turning everything into huge piles of rubble. The noise and shock of the impact are tremendous. At the same instant the explosion occurs, enormous fireballs, with surface temperatures greater than the sun's, flash across millions of acres of land, incinerating anyone not killed by the blast concussion and setting off a series of firestorms that strip the earth bare, searing all wildlife, plants, and trees.

Many U.S. missile bases are destroyed before their weapons can be launched in counterattack.

Within minutes, a second wave of nuclear warheads rains down on major metropolitan areas—New York, Washington, D.C., Chicago, Philadelphia, Los Angeles, Cleveland, Detroit, Houston, Dallas, and dozens of other cities. In seconds, tall

■ 3

buildings shatter and crash to the ground, as if a chain of mammoth earthquakes had all hit at once.

Millions of people are killed instantly by the concussions and fireballs. More are crushed under tons of debris that spew across square miles of each city. Those who huddle in shelters and survive the blast itself die of asphyxiation, as a result of oxygen depletion caused by the firestorms. Countless more die of shock or as a result of the panic. Motorists run over people in the streets and crash into each other or into buildings. Thousands are trampled to death as hordes of people run about blindly, screaming and terrified. Thousands more, their bodies mangled or horribly burned, die because there is no medical help available.

Near the epicenters, even those who live through the initial blasts and fires survive only a few hours or days more. Exposed to immense amounts of high-energy gamma radiation, they soon die of acute radiation sickness.

For those in rural areas of the country, not near targeted cities, the initial hope for survival is soon dispelled by the reality. Great clouds of radiation begin fanning out and down, carried by the prevailing wind currents. As these clouds move, they contaminate food, water, and air, polluting the country with deadly poisons.

In the weeks and months that follow, bacteria, viruses, and disease-bearing insects spread the radioactivity even farther. Surviving Americans, their natural immune processes weakened by exposure to excessive radiation, fall prey to a variety of infectious diseases. Sweeping plagues of typhoid, dysentery, polio, and other maladies run rampant and unchecked, killing large numbers of people.

More subtle are the psychological effects of the nuclear strikes. For many, the loss of family and friends and the trauma of facing life in an environmentally ruined land is too

**A Minuteman missile
in its underground silo**

much. Severe mental breakdowns result. Many people take their own lives.

The long-term future is equally grim. The blanketing radio-active fallout will cause yet more tragedies in years to come. Within five years, for example, leukemia will strike down many of the remaining survivors. Within fifteen to twenty years, others will suffer painful cancers of the stomach, bowels, lungs, breasts, and thyroid gland. Others exposed to the waves of fallout will be rendered sterile, incapable of reproduction.

For years after the blasts, horribly scarred and mutilated men, women, and children will be left to roam the land aim-lessly. America as we have known it will cease to exist. It will be reduced to less than half its population, with a large percentage of the survivors hopelessly crippled or sick. Great cities will lie under towering piles of rubble, probably never to rise again.

2

IT CAN HAPPEN

The events described in the preceding chapter may seem exaggerated. *They aren't.* Perhaps you believe that such an event could not occur. But the unfortunate truth is that it could, and at any moment. We live today atop a gigantic armed and cocked nuclear bomb. Any number of incidents, accidental or otherwise, could detonate it. It could happen today, tomorrow, next year—any time in the future. And the frightening fact is that should an all-out nuclear war be set off, the horrible scenes just described could all too quickly become stark reality.

This is because of the worldwide spread of nuclear technology and the buildup of nuclear arsenals in the years since the first atomic bomb was exploded, in the mid-1940s. Today a number of nations possess such weapons, more are developing them, and two nations—the United States and the Soviet Union—each possess arsenals so large and powerful that they could effectively blow up the entire world many times over.

Today's sophisticated weapons are far more devastating than earlier ones were. The bomb that fell on Hiroshima, for example, killed 100,000 people. Yet the United States now has nuclear warheads totaling more than 615,000 *times* the power of the Hiroshima bomb. This alone is equal to two or three tons of TNT for every person on earth.

Put another way, by various estimates the Hiroshima bomb equaled 13,000 to 20,000 tons of conventional explosives. Today, according to some calculations, the United States has nuclear warheads equivalent to 4.2 *billion* tons of explosives.

"There is now loose on the face of the earth enough nuclear might to theoretically destroy 110 billion people, or twenty seven times the present world population," Congressman Paul Simon of Illinois says.

What would happen in an all-out nuclear war if the Soviet Union attacked the United States, and the American forces struck back? Again, estimates of the number of dead vary from expert to expert, but all projections are so awesomely high that they almost defy belief.

In 1975, James R. Schlesinger, then secretary of defense, presented data on this subject to the Senate Foreign Relations Committee. He said that a Soviet attack limited to U.S. strategic forces alone would produce fatalities "on the order of five or six million" people. However, if the Soviet Union followed this up with an attack on U.S. cities, Schlesinger said, a total of 96 million Americans would die. A later study concluded that even Schlesinger's estimates were too low— far too low.

One professional group, called Physicians for Social Responsibility, calculated the destructive results of a 20-megaton (equal to 20 million tons of TNT) missile attack on one American city. They chose Boston as their example. Reporting their projections in the *New England Journal of Medicine,* they said such an attack would cause "awesome blast damage, the even more devastating thermal radiation and subsequent fire storm, the prompt and delayed radiation effects, the hopelessness of medical rescue in the face of near total destruction of medical resources, and the 1.5 million living casualties with horrible burns and trauma, radiation sickness, and raging infections."

Another group that has studied the possible effects of a nuclear attack is the 92,000-member Union of Concerned Scientists. They have reported that the Soviet Union could destroy the United States by striking 71 of the country's 119 largest metropolitan areas. Even this would not be an "all-out" attack. In fact, it would use up only about 10 percent of the Soviet's total nuclear arsenal. Yet such an attack, the group calculated, would kill half the U.S. population within thirty days and injure tens of millions. Two thirds of the nation's industrial capacity and 98 percent of its key industries would be destroyed as well.

Bernard T. Feld, a physicist at the Massachusetts Institute of Technology, writing in the *Bulletin of the Atomic Scientists,* adds, "The major damage [from such a nuclear attack] would be from huge amounts of fallout rather than from heat and direct blast devastation." Such lethal fallout would cover an immense area.

Feld predicted that a strike on U.S. land-based missiles in the western United States alone would probably involve a total of 5,000 megatons, or the equivalent of 5 trillion tons of TNT. This, he said, would produce deadly radiation fallout over a 5 million square mile area—roughly 1½ times the area of the entire United States.

However, even if all U.S. land-based nuclear weapons were knocked out, a retaliatory strike could be launched against the Soviet Union. Studies have projected that the United States, by hitting back with submarine-launched nuclear missiles and nuclear bombs carried by B-52 aircraft, could wipe out all but the smallest Soviet towns. Twenty to a hundred million Russians could be killed, depending on how the targets were selected.

But these statistics are only for the period immediately following an attack and a counterattack, a few weeks at most. The longer-term effects are much harder to assess.

Detailed studies of the survivors of the Hiroshima and Nagasaki bombings show that people exposed to radiation fallout had a much higher number of cancer deaths than normal. Many of the children who lived through the Japanese blasts developed leukemia, and there were many more cases than normal of birth defects and retarded growth among the children of mothers who were pregnant at the time of the bombings.

Further, no one can be sure that there will be *any* long-term survivors on earth following a full-scale nuclear war. Many nations, even some continents, may not be touched by the missile detonations themselves. But the great, towering clouds of radiation fallout, riding on wind currents, could eventually blanket the world. In some cases it might be months, even years, before remote areas were affected by the radiation. It is possible that some regions would be bypassed altogether, but no one knows for sure. Even if an entire continent survived, it would be like an island in a massive sea of destruction and death everywhere else.

What is known is that there are enough nuclear weapons in the world, primed and ready for firing, to virtually destroy the earth as we know it today.

How did the world get itself into such a precarious position?

3

THE ARMS RACE BEGINS

What led to the nuclear arms race as we know it today? When and why did it begin?

The answers to these questions lie in history, specifically the years surrounding the end of World War II.

During the war years, the United States was allied with many other nations in a common effort to defeat the Germans and the Japanese. One of these allies was the Soviet Union.

When the war ended in 1945, the Soviet–U.S. alliance began to collapse. The two countries moved in different directions. In the United States, for example, there was a great reduction in military strength. Most men and women in the services were discharged and returned to civilian life. Wartime factories, which had produced tanks, airplanes, and weapons, were converted back to the manufacture of peacetime products.

The Soviet Union, however, did not disband its military forces. Instead, it saw an opportunity to spread the growth of communism, particularly among the weaker nations of Eastern Europe. Even before World War II had ended, the Soviets had already annexed the Baltic states of Estonia, Latvia, and Lithuania; parts of Poland, Finland, and Romania; and eastern Czechoslovakia. And, as part of the postwar agreement with the Allies, the Soviet Union was to temporarily occupy Bulgaria, Hungary, Poland, Romania, and one third of Germany.

Steadily, the Soviets began to take control of these lands. Communist governments were organized in Albania, Bulgaria, and Romania in 1946, in Hungary and Poland in 1947, and in Czechoslovakia in 1948. All of these nations became Russian "satellites," that is, countries controlled by governments loyal to the Soviet Communist party.

As its control of these countries began to harden, the Soviet Union started sealing them off from Western Europe, in some cases putting up actual physical barricades and walls along national borders. Winston Churchill, the famous British statesman, called this sealing off of Eastern Europe an "Iron Curtain."

It became apparent to the West that the Soviets were not using their power to help nations ravaged by the war to recover. Rather, they were using it to take control of these lands and impose their political beliefs on them, whether the people wanted it or not.

Realizing this, the Allies, led by the United States, Britain, and France, established a plan to declare that part of Germany not under Russian control an independent country. Thus was born West Germany.

Berlin, the former capital of Germany, lay completely within the Soviet zone, but parts of it were under Western control. The Russians, hoping to "freeze out" the Allies in the city, closed off its borders to all rail and highway transportation, which had been used to supply Berlin with food and other essentials. However, the Allies began an airlift in 1948, sending in necessary supplies by plane. The airlift lasted nearly a year before the Russians, realizing the blockade had failed, finally reopened the borders to traffic, and West Berlin eventually became part of West Germany.

All during the early postwar years, tension and mutual distrust were building between the Soviet Union and the Western allied nations. To protect themselves against what they called capitalistic aggression, the Russians, and later the Chinese, encouraged the formation of Communist dictatorships in the countries around them. They believed that in time all countries would succumb to communism. The Western nations sought to preserve a democratic way of life, believing in individual freedom and a government representative of the people. They also believed that the free enterprise system was the best way to raise living standards.

Both sides, unable to settle their differences through negotiation, built up their military arms. This became known as the Cold War, so called because there was no actual fighting going on, but each side, fearful of the other, built up its defenses to be prepared in case actual war should break out.

These, then, are some of the reasons why the arms race began, leading to the dire nuclear threat that hangs heavy over the world today. It is particularly unfortunate that events happened the way they did, because there was a brief period immediately following the end of World War II when the arms race, especially the proliferation of nuclear weapons, might have been halted shortly after its birth.

This opportunity arose with the creation of the United Nations in June 1945. The very first resolution of the new international body, by unanimous decision of the member nations, called for the establishment of an Atomic Energy Commission. This commission was charged with the urgent responsibility of making specific proposals "for the elimination from national armaments of atomic weapons and of all other major weapons adaptable to mass destruction."

The timing seemed right for such action. Only three bombs had thus far been exploded—one test bomb in New Mexico and the two bombs the United States had dropped on Japan near the end of the war. No other country at the time, including the Soviet Union, had the technology to build nuclear weapons.

The United States was willing to give up its advantage as the leader in the development of atomic bombs because, as a report released in 1946 stated: "the extremely favored position with regard to atomic devices, which the United States enjoys at present, is only temporary. It will not last. We must use that advantage now to promote international security and to carry out our policy of building a lasting peace through international agreement."

In line with the UN resolution, the United States drafted a plan calling for an end to the development of nuclear arms. The main author of this plan was the American financier and statesman Bernard Baruch. The plan called for prohibiting the manufacture of atomic bombs and placing all phases of the development and use of atomic energy under an international authority. It was presented to the UN Atomic Energy Commission on June 14, 1946.

The Russians, however, rejected the plan, saying it placed unfair restrictions upon them. They also distrusted any plan that would be administered by the UN because they felt the United States really controlled the UN. On top of this, the United States exploded another test bomb over Bikini Atoll in the Pacific Ocean on July 1, 1946, even before some of the commission's subcommittees had met to discuss the plan.

Further, the Soviets wanted the United States to share its technical knowledge with the international agency, and the United States was not willing to do this. Many attempts were made to settle the various disagreements, but the two major powers, the Soviet Union and the United States, would not alter their positions.

Consequently, the plan was doomed to failure, and when the Soviets exploded their first test atomic bomb in 1949, in the midst of the escalating Cold War, all real hopes of banning nuclear weapons were lost. The arms race was on in earnest.

4

SOVIET MILITARY STRENGTH

For a number of years after the end of World War II, the United States was the only superpower in the world. No other nation on earth could come close to matching its great military strength. The United States had a commanding lead in weapons, skills, and technology.

Today this is no longer true. Over the past two and a half decades, the Soviet Union has directed a larger percentage of its resources to the building and development of military power than has the United States or any other nation. As a consequence of this emphasis, the Soviet Union currently has a strength near, equal to, or perhaps even superior to, that of the United States. Experts disagree on just how strong the Soviet Union has become in relation to America's forces.

One who believes that the Soviet Union has surpassed the United States is Senator Henry Jackson of the state of Washington. "In 1969," the senator says, "the United States led the Soviet Union in every single indicator of strategic military strength: the number of land-based and sea-based missiles, the number of warheads, the megatonnage of its missile force, the accuracy of its weapons, the potential of its missiles to strike protected military targets, and so forth.

"Now, the Soviet Union leads the United States in every one of these same indicators with only one exception, the number of warheads. And the American lead in warheads is rapidly evaporating," Jackson adds.

It is difficult to tell exactly who is "ahead" in this arms race, or whether superiority even has any real significance where nuclear weapons are involved. It is known, however, that Soviet strength has greatly increased since the 1960s because of the additional money and effort the Russians have put into their military programs. And almost all experts concede that even if the United States is still the strongest nation in the world today, its once commanding lead has been shaved razor thin.

"In 1979, the Soviet military effort was about 50 percent larger than our own," says former U.S. Secretary of Defense Harold Brown. "In strategic nuclear forces, the Soviets have come from a position of substantial numerical inferiority fifteen years ago to one of parity [equality] today," Brown adds.

Each of the superpowers—the Soviet Union and the United States—has three main categories of military strength: strategic nuclear forces; tactical or theater nuclear forces; and conventional forces.

Strategic Nuclear Forces

Strategic nuclear forces are made up of a wide range of the most powerful weapons, including missiles and bomber aircraft armed with nuclear warheads. It is these types of arsenals that would be used in an all-out strike, as described in Chapter 1.

The Soviet Union has three main groups of strategic nuclear weapons. The first are the intercontinental ballistic missiles (ICBMs). They are land-based missiles armed with multiple nuclear warheads that are capable, as their name implies, of traveling thousands of miles to hit targets on another continent with incredible accuracy.

Currently, the Soviets have about 1,400 ICBM launchers. More than 650 of these, or nearly half, are equipped with MIRVs. (MIRV stands for multiple independently targetable reentry vehicle.) Thus, a MIRVed ICBM can be launched with several warheads instead of just one. In 1964, the year a Defense Department report measuring Soviet growth was issued, the Russians had only 190 ICBMs. Thus it is obvious that they have, over the years, put a great deal of emphasis on the buildup of these long-range weapons.

The ICBM launchers are located at "fixed" sites. They cannot be moved from one base to another at the present time. It is believed that the Soviets could develop a mobile ICBM–launching capability, but that they have chosen not to at the present time. Mobile launchers would be more difficult to destroy in an all-out nuclear strike.

The second group of strategic nuclear arms that the Soviets have placed great emphasis on are the SLBMs—submarine-launched ballistic missiles. They now have 950 SLBMs. In 1964 they had only 29. SLBMs are deployed on fleets of nuclear-powered submarines that prowl the world's oceans. The Soviets have more than 60 such submarines. More than 100 of the SLBMs are MIRVed.

Nuclear-armed missiles on submarines are, of course, much harder to hit because of their maneuverability and their ability to "hide" beneath the seas. SLBMs, like ICBMs, have the capability of striking targets great distances away with effective accuracy. Submarines stationed in the Atlantic or Pacific Ocean, for instance, could easily reach any target in the United States or on the North American continent.

The third group within the Soviet strategic nuclear force is made up of bomber aircraft. This is the only group that has not been greatly expanded in recent years. In fact, in 1964, the Soviets had 170 such aircraft. Today their long-range bomber force consists of 156 Bison and Bear aircraft. Each is capable of launching nuclear warheads.

The Soviets have, however, developed a new bomber—the Backfire—in the past decade. Although it is generally believed by U.S. military experts that this aircraft was not designed for intercontinental range, it still has the capability of reaching U.S. targets if used on one-way high-altitude flights.

The total strategic nuclear force of the Soviet Union, including ICBMs, SLBMs, and long-range bombers, now numbers 6,000 nuclear warheads. In 1964 the Soviets had only 400.

These are all offensive weapons. The Soviets also have strategic defensive forces that could be used if they were attacked with nuclear weapons. They have very sophisticated radar systems to detect a nuclear attack and also 2,600 interceptor aircraft plus about 10,000 SAM (surface-to-air missile) launchers that could all be deployed during an attack in an effort to destroy incoming missiles and bombers.

Tactical or Theater Nuclear Forces
This category of forces includes less powerful weapons systems that cannot go the distances achieved by the strategic nuclear forces. Such weapons would be used for close-range targets such as those in Western Europe. Tactical weapons based in Siberia could reach any part of Asia.

There is actually greater concern among U.S. and Western European military leaders over the possibility of a "limited" nuclear war than of an all-out strike using the most powerful nuclear weapons. Much of U.S. defense planning for the past thirty-five years has been dominated less by the possibility of a surprise attack with strategic weapons on the United States than by the threat of a massive Soviet invasion of Western Europe.

To build a deterrent strong enough to discourage this threat, the United States and many Western European nations in 1949 formed an alliance called NATO (North Atlantic Treaty Organization). Under NATO, each member nation contributes manpower, money, and arms to maintain a strong overall defense program.

To counter NATO, the Soviet Union in 1955 created an alliance of its own, the Warsaw Pact, which includes the USSR and six other Eastern European nations under Soviet domination.

The Soviet theater nuclear force, like its strategic nuclear force, has been greatly strengthened and modernized over the past several years. Said former Secretary Brown in 1980: "The Soviets, by now, have deployed large numbers of theater-oriented nuclear delivery systems, and we believe they have stockpiled sufficient warheads to supply these systems."

Theater nuclear attack forces based in the Soviet Union include more than 450 intermediate-range Badger and Blinder bomber aircraft and about 60 Backfire bombers. The Russians also have over 400 medium-range and intermediate-range ballistic missiles, plus more than 100 mobile intermediate-range ballistic missile launchers, each of them carrying three MIRVs.

The intermediate-range ballistic missiles and the Backfire bombers are gradually replacing older missiles and bombers. The Soviets are producing 30 new Backfires a year. The Backfire carries more weapons and can penetrate enemy defenses better than the older bombers.

The newest intermediate-range ballistic missiles are more mobile and are therefore more difficult to hit as targets. Their range is greater, and each of the three warheads on board is far more accurate than the older missiles were. In addition, the Soviets have older submarine fleets in the Baltic and North seas armed with ballistic missiles capable of striking any point in Western Europe.

Of the 100 new Soviet intermediate-range missile launchers, 60 are in the European theater. That is, they are positioned to strike targets in Western Europe should a war break out. Forty of the 60 Backfire bombers also are in the European theater, as are all of the older missile launchers and 350 of the 450 or so older bombers. All of these missiles and bombers have the range capability to strike any target on the European continent.

Further, U.S. defense experts estimate the Soviets will have 150 to 200 more missile launchers and 40 to 90 more Backfire aircraft available by the mid-1980s.

All members of the Warsaw Pact continue to equip and

■ 19

train their forces to operate in chemical and nuclear environments. They also continue to improve their capabilities for the actual use of chemical weapons, which include poison gases.

Conventional Forces

These forces, including land, sea, and air force weapons and manpower, are nonnuclear. Here, again, the Russians have greatly added to their strength over the past fifteen years. "In conventional weapons, the situation is also serious," says Senator Henry Jackson. "The Soviets lead us in tanks by five to one, in artillery pieces by 2.3 to one, in attack submarines by 3.5 to one, in ground forces divisions by 10 to one, and in medium bombers by 11 to one."

It is estimated that the Soviet army now has 55,000 tanks. The United States has 11,000. The Russians also lead in armored troop carriers, 55,000 to 17,600; in artillery pieces, 22,000 to 5,600; in total aircraft of all kinds, 8,800 to 6,400; and in total naval ships, 1,769 to about 450.

In the mid-1960s, Soviet land and tactical air forces consisted of about 1.4 million men. They have now expanded to over 2 million men, not including 450,000 border guards and internal security units with military capabilities.

Much of this expansion has resulted from a military buildup along the Soviet-Chinese border. Here alone, the forces grew from 20 divisions and 210 fighter aircraft in 1965 to 46 divisions and 1,200 fighter aircraft in 1979. Even so, approximately 154,000 men have been added during the past eleven years to the Soviet forces stationed in Eastern Europe.

Furthermore, over the past fifteen years, the Soviet army has been re-equipped with more modern tanks, improved armored infantry fighting vehicles, self-propelled artillery, and new battlefield missiles.

This buildup includes the relatively modern T-62 and the newer T-64 tanks; the BMP armored fighting vehicle; heavy, mobile, multiple-rocket launchers; and the self-propelled armored versions of the 122-millimeter and 152-millimeter artillery guns. Air defenses have also been modernized. They rely on new antiaircraft guns and five types of mobile surface-to-air missiles.

Overall, since 1965, the Soviets have increased the total number of their divisions from 148 to over 170 and have added 1,400 aircraft and 31 regiments to their tactical air armies. According to recent Defense Department reports, Soviet ground forces today consist of roughly 1.8 million men organized into three types of divisions: motorized rifle divisions; tank divisions; and airborne divisions.

It is estimated that about 900,000 of these troops are released from active duty each year. This means that in addition to the present strength, the Soviets also have a pool of about 4 million men, from over the past five years, with military experience in the ground forces.

The total Soviet tactical air force consists of approximately 4,500 first-line combat aircraft. In addition, 500 Badger intermediate-range bombers and some Backfire long-range bombers could be used for conventional warfare. The Russians continue to upgrade their air armies with late-model Fishbed MIG-21s, Flogger MIG-23s and 27s, Fitter SU-17s, and Fencer SU-24s. These aircraft have greater range and carry heavier weapon loads than older aircraft now being phased out of operations. There are, in addition, another 600 medium- and long-range transport planes.

The Russian navy, once considered weak, has also been growing rapidly. The oceangoing surface warship force now includes

- 2 guided missile carriers and a third being built;
- 2 guided missile aviation cruisers;
- 269 other surface warships, including 19 with anti-ship missile launchers;
- a number of additional large warships in various stages of construction.

■ 21

Additionally, the Soviets have a fleet of 205 attack submarines and 65 cruise missile submarines. Some of these craft can launch anti-ship missiles while submerged.

There are also 91 amphibious warfare ships, some capable of open-ocean travel, which can transport thousands of troops. Another fleet of nearly 300 ships, including tankers and supply vessels, supports the warships.

5

U.S. MILITARY STRENGTH

Despite the dramatic progress the Soviets have made over the past twenty years, most experts still consider the United States the strongest military power on earth. However, as mentioned earlier, it is acknowledged that because the Soviet Union has placed far more emphasis, effort, and money on development of its military capabilities since the 1960s than the United States has, the once-great lead in overall strength held by the United States has narrowed to a very slim margin.

American defense programs have not always been given the highest priorities. In fact, American military manpower has been reduced since the end of the Vietnam War, while Soviet forces have steadily increased.

Historically, the United States was the first nation to develop nuclear weapons. Their enormous destructive power was first demonstrated with the bombings of Hiroshima and Nagasaki in 1945, which hastened the end of World War II. Through the years the United States has built and maintained a massive arsenal of weapons.

TITAN SS-7 SS-8 Minuteman II SS-11 SS-9 Minuteman III SS-13 SS

←——————— 1960 — 1965 ———————→ ←——————— 1965 — 1970 ———————→

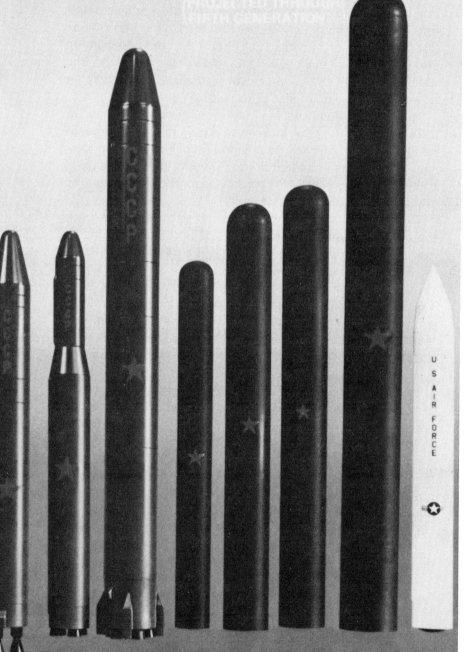

NTAL BALLISTIC MISSILES
(PROJECTED THROUGH
FIFTH GENERATION)

| SS-19 | SS-17 | SS-18 | Symbolic of Fifth Generation | MX |

| 1970 — 1975 | UNDER DEVELOPMENT |

Strategic Nuclear Forces

It is generally believed in the United States that a strong military is needed to balance world power by serving as a deterrent. That is, if an enemy knows that the United States is as strong as it is, or stronger, and that it has the capability of striking back in nuclear attack, blow for blow, then the enemy is less likely to start a war. It realizes it would suffer as much or more in retaliation for such an attack.

The U.S. strategic nuclear force is based on a triad, or three-pronged, concept of defense. This includes intercontinental ballistic missiles, submarine-launched ballistic missiles, and manned bomber aircraft. Each of these three parts of the triad is capable of raining widespread devastation on any point on earth.

The triad concept, which the Soviets also use, is based on the belief that an attacking enemy could knock out one or even two of the defensive legs, but not all three. This leaves the enemy open to massive counterattack.

At present, the United States has 1,054 land-based ICBMs. These include 450 Minuteman IIs, each armed with a single warhead; 550 Minuteman IIIs, each capable of placing warheads on three widely separated targets; and 54 Titan II ICBMs. The advantages of this force include a low cost to operate, the ability to launch quickly in response to an enemy attack, endurance, and a high degree of accuracy. All of these missiles can travel across oceans or continents to reach any enemy target.

A large number of the Minuteman IIIs are being refitted with new, more advanced MK12A warheads. This will give them the capability of destroying enemy missile sites sheltered by hard concrete or other materials. Eventually, 300 Minuteman IIIs will receive this warhead.

Of great concern to U.S. military experts is the belief that the Russians are developing missiles with warheads that could destroy the American ICBM force, now housed in permanent underground silos in several states, mostly in the West.

To counter this threat, the United States is considering a new ICBM system called MX. Under one concept of this program, many sites would be built in the western United States, and the missiles could be shuttled from site to site over a modern rail system. Thus, an enemy would not know at which sites the active ICBMs would be located at any given time, thereby greatly decreasing the chances of destroying them. Specifically, 200 MX missiles would be shuttled back and forth between 4,600 underground shelters situated in about 40 remote desert valleys.

The MX system would also have greatly increased accuracy and would carry larger numbers of reentry vehicles. Warheads being considered for the MX could deploy from eight to ten MIRVs.

The submarine-launched ballistic missile force includes missiles deployed on 41 submarines. There are 496 Poseidon C-3 or Trident I missiles on 31 Poseidon submarines and 160 Polaris missiles on 10 Polaris subs; and new Trident subs, each carrying 24 Trident missiles, will soon replace some of the older Polaris and Poseidon submarines.

The Poseidon missile can carry up to 14 MIRVs. The Trident submarines, which began to enter service in 1981, can each carry 24 MIRVed missiles. The greater effectiveness and higher survival rate of the Trident subs will contribute to a strong sea-based deterrent through the rest of the century and possibly beyond. The Trident is quieter and faster, can stay at sea longer, and is armed with longer-range missiles that can go up to 4,600 miles (7,400 km)—considerably farther than the older Poseidon system.

The third part of the strategic nuclear triad is made up of manned bomber aircraft. The heart of this fleet consists of 316 B-52 long-range bombers, organized in 21 squadrons. This force also includes 60 FB-11 medium-range bombers, in four squadrons, and 615 K-135 tanker aircraft in 33 active and 16 reserve squadrons. The tankers can refuel the bombers in midair.

This bomber force carries approximately one third of all

Left: the underwater firing of
a Polaris missile from an
unidentified submarine. Above:
a B-52 bomber modified to carry
an air-launched cruise missile.

U.S. nuclear weapons and half the megatonnage. (A megaton is equal to 1 million tons of TNT.) About 30 percent of the B-52s and other aircraft are maintained on a day-to-day alert system. That is, these planes can be en route to enemy targets within minutes of being called.

The B-52s are equipped with the short-range attack missile (SRAM), a supersonic nuclear weapon that can penetrate any known enemy defense to strike prime targets.

There are two key advantages to manned bomber aircraft. One is that they are mobile. The other is that they can be called back from attack at any point in their mission should there be a false alarm or error. The land- and sea-based missiles cannot be recalled once they have been launched.

The Air Force is currently planning the addition of a force of 3,400 air-launched cruise missiles (ALCMs). The United States is considering deploying such missiles on 120 to 150 B-52s. This would virtually double the number of weapons these aircraft now carry. Launched from the bombers, the cruise missiles would further complicate enemy defenses, increasing the overall chances of making a successful counterattack. These 20-foot-long (6-m) "nuclear darts" could be launched from bombers outside the range of Russian defenses and be directed to important targets within the Soviet Union. They are designed to fly at altitudes low enough to avoid detection by normal radar equipment.

The three new major U.S. weapons development programs proposed for the 1980s—the MX missiles, the Trident nuclear submarines and missiles, and the cruise missiles—will, it is estimated by some experts, cost approximately $70 billion over the decade if they are all approved.

Counting all the independently targetable weapons in the ICBMs, SLBMs, and manned bomber aircraft, the United States now has approximately 9,200 nuclear warheads and bombs in its strategic arsenal.

In strategic defensive forces, the United States does not have an active ballistic missile defense system. Rather, air defense of North America is dependent upon 108 active-duty manned interceptor aircraft, 165 Air National Guard manned interceptors, and 7 airborne warning and control system (AWACS) aircraft. The interceptors include F-4, F-101, and F-106 aircraft. An additional 18 interceptors in Alaska and two Canadian squadrons of 36 manned interceptors add up to 334 combat-ready aircraft.

The first and most important signals in the U.S. defense system to sound an alert of an enemy attack, nuclear of conventional, will come from a network of early-warning satellites positioned in earth orbit. Following this, the ballistic missile early warning system (BMEWS) and the submarine-launched ballistic missile radar warning system would confirm such an attack. Another series of radar systems is designed to pick up and track any enemy aircraft headed for the North American continent. There is no air defense shield made up of military aircraft and antiaircraft weapons, because it is generally believed that a missile attack represents by far the more serious threat.

**Tactical or
Theater Nuclear Forces**

Since the end of World War II, U.S. military leaders have felt that the most immediate threat to the Free World would probably come through a "limited" war. They believe an all-out nuclear war is less likely because of the balance of power.

However, because the Soviet Union is close enough geographically to cast a "long shadow" across all of Western Europe, U.S. military leaders have stressed planning defenses for an invasion of that area. This was the thinking behind the creation of NATO in 1949. Such a limited war, it was believed, would include the use of some tactical nuclear weapons. (NATO members today include Belgium, Canada, Denmark, France, Greece, Iceland, Italy, Luxembourg, the Netherlands, Norway, Portugal, Turkey, the United Kingdom, the United States, and West Germany.)

NATO forces, largely supplied with U.S. hardware and technology, include a wide variety of theater nuclear and nonnuclear weapons. In fact, the United States deploys about 7,000 nuclear weapons and more than 200,000 troops in support of NATO in Europe. Many additional thousands of such weapons are positioned at other sites around the world.

Short-range systems—those that can strike targets within 60 miles (100 km)—include such artillery as 155-mm and 8-inch howitzers, which fire atomic projectiles, and the Lance missile. However, a number of these weapons, especially the artillery ones, are getting old, and their effectiveness as a deterrent is lessening.

The U.S.–built Pershing missile is used by NATO as a medium-range weapon. It can hit targets at a distance of 600 miles (960 km). Other medium-range systems include "dual capable" aircraft, such as the F-4, F-16, and Tornado fighters. "Dual capable" means they can be equipped to fire either nuclear or nonnuclear weapons. Older nuclear bombs that can be carried by these aircraft are being replaced by more efficient B-61 bombs.

U.S. contributions of long-range weapons in the NATO theater nuclear force include the F-111 fighter-bomber and the A-6 aircraft. A substantial number of Poseidon reentry vehicles can also be used in NATO defense forces in case of enemy attack. They would be launched from nuclear submarines.

To keep NATO systems current, and thus keep their deterrent value strong, a number of new long-range weapons are now being considered for development. These include air-, sea-, and land-launched cruise missiles, a new medium-range ballistic missile, and more and better aircraft.

In naval systems, the United States is planning a nuclear warhead for its Harpoon anti-ship missile, which is designed to strike attacking ships at sea.

Conventional Forces

The United States currently has slightly more than 2 million men and women in its armed forces. This is about 1.5 million less than during the height of the Vietnam War in the late 1960s.

Army and Marine Corps land forces are the only military forces capable of holding or retaking territory. They form the mainstay of conventional forces. These land forces are designed primarily to act as part of the NATO alliance in countering Soviet and Warsaw Pact ground forces in Europe. While most emphasis is on the defense of Europe, other ground units can respond rapidly to any crisis anywhere in the world.

At present, the United States has 28 divisions. Of these, 19 are active, including 16 Army and 3 Marine Corps divisions. There are also 9 Reserve Component divisions—8 Army National Guard and 1 Marine Corps.

The Army and Marine Corps have a total of 11,000 tanks. Most of these are M-60s, a model that has been in service since the 1960s. They will continue in use until about 1990. An improved version, the M-60A1, has been designed to increase reliability, durability, firepower, mobility, and night-fighting capability.

A new tank, the XM-1, is now being produced and eventually will replace the older M-60. Initially armed with a 105-mm main gun, the XM-1 will be fitted with a larger, more powerful 120-mm gun starting in 1984. The Army plans to purchase more than 350 of these improved tanks.

Aside from tanks, the U.S. Army has no armored fighting vehicle as such, but relies on the lightly armored, mobile M-113 personnel carrier to transport troops into battle. A new amored Infantry/Cavalry Fighting Vehicle is designed to replace the M-113 in mechanized tank and cavalry units. Its main armament consists of the TOW antitank missile and a 25-mm automatic dual-feed cannon.

In recent years the helicopter has become a more important weapon, with ground forces supplying an added degree of mobility and firepower. Here, the United States has a clear lead over the Soviet Union. The U.S. Army has 7,800 helicopters; the Soviets have about 3,500.

The AH-1S Cobra helicopter is armed with the TOW antitank missile system. The UH-60A Blackhawk is now replacing older UH-1 Huey helicopters for air assault, air cavalry, and airborne medical evacuation roles. A newer system is the AAH (advanced attack helicopter). It is a twin-engine rotary-wing vehicle armed with the Hellfire antitank missile, a 30-mm cannon, and 2.75-inch rockets.

In artillery, the United States depends on the M-198 towed 155-mm howitzer and the M-109A2 self-propelled howitzer. A number of improved, longer-range artillery fire systems are under development. In antitank weapons, the U.S. Army and Marine Corps use the TOW weapon, which can destroy most enemy tanks, armored vehicles, and field fortifications at a range of up to 9,900 feet (3,000 m). The Dragon is another antitank guided missile system.

The United States plans to spend more than $8 billion over the next five years to improve its aging air defense system. The current Nike Hercules and the basic Hawk surface-to-air systems are from fifteen to twenty-five years old and are costly to operate and maintain. As a result, the basic Hawk has been replaced by the Improved Hawk system.

In the 1980s, however, both the Improved Hawk and the Nike Hercules are to be replaced by the Patriot. Each Patriot firing section will be able to engage a number of targets at the same time.

Two new air defense weapons have also entered production and will be available for development in the near future. The Stinger, an individual shoulder-fired missile, will replace the older Redeye. The new radar-equipped Roland will replace Chaparral. Another new air defense weapon is the Divad gun. It is a radar-directed air defense gun system with either 35- or 40-mm twin cannons in an armored enclosure, mounted on a tracked vehicle.

U.S. naval general-purpose forces are designed to carry out six warfare tasks. These are strike warfare; antisubmarine warfare; antiair warfare; anti-surface warfare; mine warfare; and amphibious warfare.

Carrier battle groups, or fleets, composed of twelve active carriers each, are the backbone of the Navy's forces. They provide the most effective means of sea control. Of these twelve carrier battle groups, three are nuclear-powered.

The antisubmarine force includes attack submarines, land-based patrol aircraft, carrier-based aircraft and helicopters, surface ships with antisubmarine capability, and destroyer- and frigate-based helicopters.

Mines are high-power explosives placed in the water to blow up enemy ships. U.S. mines are based on designs twenty years old, are difficult and expensive to maintain, and have only limited value today against attack surface ships and high-speed targets. The Navy is developing a new family of mines.

The Navy is also modernizing its amphibious craft, which are used to transport troops from the sea to landings. Two new landing craft are the LHA and the LSD-41, which will be able to land on beaches that older craft couldn't reach.

The U.S. conventional Air Force is built around use of the A-10, F-15, and F-16 fighter aircraft. The A-10 is designed especially for close air support missions and can destroy enemy armored vehicles and tanks. It has Maverick missiles, Rockeye 30-mm ammunition, and laser-guided weapons.

The F-15 is designed for air-to-air combat, as is the F-16, which carries Sidewinder missiles. Naval air forces include the F-14, equipped with the Phoenix weapon system. The F/A-18 is a multi-mission Navy and Marine Corps aircraft for light attack roles. The A-6E aircraft furnishes close air support for the Navy and Marine Corps.

Additionally, the United States has more than 300 long-range airlift aircraft and can call on another 200-plus civilian cargo and passenger aircraft to meet defense needs during an emergency. The mainstays of this force are the C-141 and the C-5, which can ferry heavy equipment such as howitzers and tanks. The Military Sealift Command fleet is made up of 33 cargo ships and 27 tankers.

6

THE SPREAD OF NUCLEAR WEAPONS

When the United States dropped two atomic bombs on Japan in 1945, hundreds of thousands of people were killed or maimed. Recognizing the dangers of such awesome weapons, the United Nations, as early as 1946, established a commission endowed with the urgent task of making specific proposals for the elimination of such weapons of mass destruction.

Unfortunately, no such proposals were ever adopted. In the Soviet Union, scientists worked feverishly to develop their country's own nuclear arsenal. In 1949 the Russians successfully tested their first atomic bomb.

Two years later, the United States shared its world-leading technology with the United Kingdom, and in 1952 the United Kingdom exploded its first bomb, in a test on the Australian island of Monte Bello. France soon developed the bomb also, detonating its first test bomb in 1960. World leaders were very conscious of the great gap in military power between those nations that had nuclear weapons and those that didn't.

Discussions of how to keep nuclear arms from spreading even farther began at the United Nations in 1957. Four years later, in 1961, the UN General Assembly unanimously adopted an Irish resolution calling on all nations to conclude a "non-proliferation" agreement meant to stop further development of nuclear weapons by nations that did not yet possess them.

Almost every nation agreed that this was a good idea. In 1963, President John F. Kennedy, in a major speech, said, "I ask you to stop and think for a moment what it would mean to have nuclear weapons in so many hands, in the hands of countries large and small, stable and unstable, responsible and irresponsible, scattered throughout the world. There would be no rest for anyone then, no stability, no real security, and no chance of effective disarmament. There would only be the increased chance of accidental war and an increased necessity for the great powers to involve themselves in what would otherwise be local conflicts."

Even though there was general agreement among most nations on the need for nuclear restraint, there were a lot of problems to be solved and questions still to be answered.

The talks and negotiations dragged on. Meanwhile, in 1964, the People's Republic of China, not yet a member of the United Nations, exploded a nuclear bomb, bringing to five the number of countries having this capability.

The work of trying to get an acceptable non-proliferation agreement fell to the UN Commission on Disarmament. Among the major questions to be resolved were these:

■ If a nonnuclear nation signed such an agreement, would that automatically mean it would be a weaker, "second-class" nation?

■ If nonnuclear nations showed their good faith by signing a non-proliferation treaty, would the world powers that had nuclear weapons likewise take some positive steps toward reducing their arsenals?

■ If a nonnuclear nation did sign such a treaty, how would its security be assured, particularly against nations armed with nuclear weapons?

The last question was answered in June 1968, when the Security Council of the United Nations approved a resolution that, in so many words, said the United States, the United Kingdom, and the Soviet Union pledged they would come to the assistance of any nonnuclear country that was threatened by the use of nuclear weapons.

But as the many nations of the world pondered the proposed non-proliferation treaty, another thorny issue arose. What if nations used their peaceful nuclear resources for weapons? Many nations had, or would soon have access to, the technology and natural resources needed to develop nuclear energy. What safeguards would the world have that a nation would not divert such knowledge and materials to military purposes?

It was generally believed—and still is—that the possibility of nuclear war increases in direct proportion to the number of nuclear-armed nations. This would be especially true if countries that had a long history of unrest or feuding with other countries were suddenly to become nuclear powers.

This particular danger was spotlighted on June 7, 1981, when a squad of six Israeli F-16 jets boldly bombed and destroyed a nuclear reactor at El-Tuwaitha, Iraq, near Baghdad. The surprise attack created a worldwide flood of protest over the action. Israeli leaders defended the strike by declaring that the Iraqis were preparing atomic bombs at the site, intending to use them against Israel. This charge was refuted by Iraq.

There has also been over the years a growing concern about terrorist groups. In recent times such groups have stepped up attacks on nuclear power plants. What if one of these groups were to capture a nuclear bomb? It could hold the world to ransom and name its own price.

It was the question of safeguards that resulted in the formation of the International Atomic Energy Agency (IAEA) in 1957. The IAEA is a self-governing body, but it has direct reporting links with the UN General Assembly and the Security Council. The IAEA is actually an outgrowth of the "Atoms for Peace" proposal made by President Dwight D. Eisenhower in 1953, when he called for "international control of atomic energy to promote its use for peaceful purposes only . . . under adequate safeguards, including a practical system of inspection under the United Nations."

The IAEA is financed by the more than one hundred nations who are members. It has a permanent staff of about a thousand, including scientists and technicians. The techniques introduced by some of these scientists over the years to help safeguard against the spread of nuclear weapons include portable instruments to measure amounts of uranium and plutonium used in nuclear processes; tamper-proof instruments to be placed at nuclear sites for continuous monitoring; seals to be placed on doors, vaults, and containers of nuclear materials; and devices that can verify how much plutonium is produced by nuclear reactors.

With the issue of safeguards having been seriously addressed and the IAEA set up to deal with those safeguards, the Treaty on the Non-Proliferation of Nuclear Weapons was ready for signing on July 1, 1968. It became effective on March 5, 1970, when enough nations had ratified it. Today, more than a hundred nations have ratified the treaty and about twenty others have signed but not yet ratified it.

Is the treaty working? Is it effectively halting the dangerous spread of nuclear weapons? The best answer might be yes and no. The treaty is working in part, but there are some real problems. Most of the nations that do not have nuclear weapons have lived up to their agreements. But the nuclear powers have not.

A specific sore point among the nonnuclear nations is Article 6 of the treaty, which calls for a commitment by states that have nuclear weapons to work toward nuclear disarmament. There have been some forward steps taken—notably a limited ban on testing of nuclear weapons and work toward a ceiling on the total number of strategic nuclear weapons possessed by the United States and the Soviet Union.

However, there has been general disappointment at the disarmament progress made over the past decade by these two superpowers. The arms race, in fact, continued right through the 1970s and early 1980s, with both the United States and the Soviet Union continuing to build and refine their nuclear arsenals.

Such a direction by the two strongest nations on earth sets a poor example for others to follow. Many of the nonnuclear nations that have kept their promise not to acquire nuclear weapons feel cheated. They feel that this continued buildup further widens the gap between nuclear and nonnuclear nations. Several countries—China, India, Algeria, and Argentina, among others—have refused to adopt the treaty for this very reason.

France, a nuclear-armed nation, also did not ratify the treaty, but did say it would "behave in the future exactly as did the states that did ratify it." China, though, made no such promise. Fearful of the Soviet Union, China said it felt compelled to develop its own arsenal of nuclear weapons for the purpose of self-defense and "to break the nuclear monopoly and blackmail of the superpowers."

In May 1980, China successfully test-launched an intercontinental ballistic missile, which came down in the South Pacific Ocean. This action indicated that China now had a capability to fire nuclear weapons that could reach any part of the Soviet Union and the West Coast of the United States.

The non-proliferation picture was further complicated in 1974 when India became the sixth nation on earth to explode a nuclear bomb. Although India said the test was strictly for "peaceful purposes," it nevertheless demonstrated that the nation now at least had the technology to build a nuclear arsenal. At the time, the U.S. ambassador to the United Nations, Joseph Martin, Jr., commented, "It is clearly impossible to develop a capability to conduct nuclear explosions for peaceful purposes without, in the process, acquiring a device which could be used as a nuclear weapon."

Furthermore, a number of other nations, including Argentina, Brazil, Egypt, Iraq, Israel, and South Africa, have or are acquiring the necessary technology and the basic materials to build nuclear weapons in the near future, and many believe that Israel may already have such weapons.

Despite these developments, however, the nations that have ratified the nuclear non-proliferation treaty are still hopeful that the remaining problems can be solved and that the treaty will become a binding, effective force to control the spread of nuclear weaponry.

When the treaty was drawn up, it was determined that every five years there should be a review conference of the members who had ratified the treaty. The first such conference met in 1975 and the second one in 1980. Prior to this second conference, a preparatory committee met, and some of its findings offered some real hope for the future success of the treaty. The committee called the treaty the "centerpiece of international arrangements, providing a framework in which cooperation in the peaceful uses of nuclear energy can proceed without fear that it will lead to the spread of nuclear weapons. It provides the vehicle through which the overwhelming majority of states have made binding legal commitments to each other that they will not acquire or produce nuclear weapons."

The committee pointed out that such commitments were supported by a safeguard system designed to see that no such weapons were being developed and that the success of this system "provides the assurance which the international community must have if cooperation in the peaceful uses of nuclear energy is to proceed with confidence."

The committee said that over a hundred nations were now under the treaty and more were joining. It felt that this would put added pressure on those countries that "remain outside the treaty to think about acquiring nuclear weapons."

In 1979, six additional countries—Indonesia, Sri Lanka, Bangladesh, the People's Republic of Yemen, Tuvalu, and the Cape Verde Islands—became parties to the treaty, bringing the total number to 114.

Finally, the committee stated that universal acceptance of the treaty would "of course not only provide the highest possible degree of assurance against proliferation, but would also speed wider cooperation in the peaceful uses of nuclear energy."

7

EARLY ATTEMPTS TO HALT THE ARMS RACE

People have tried to limit the use of weapons in war through-out history. Attempts have been made to outlaw war and to create means of settling disputes through peaceful negotia-tion. Nations have tried to avert war by withdrawing into iso-lation or neutrality, or by joining with others in leagues or alliances for the common defense of all the member nations. However, through the centuries, most of these efforts have proved unsuccessful.

There have been a few exceptions. In 1817, for instance, the United States and Britain agreed to limit their rival naval forces on the Great Lakes to a few vessels on each side.

Several nations joined in setting up the International Peace Conferences at The Hague in the Netherlands in 1899 and 1907. Here, leaders made some advances in clarifying the "rules of war" and in establishing a means for settling disputes through the Permanent Court of Arbitration, which was a forerunner to the present International Court of Justice.

At the 1899 conference, the nations signed a declaration banning the use of dumdum bullets and poison gases, and the launching of explosives and projectiles from balloons. At the 1907 meeting, the use of mines and torpedoes was prohibited.

The Hague conferences were, in fact, the first attempts to take an international approach to the problems of war and peace. There was much interest in these proceedings because the Industrial Revolution of the late nineteenth century, as a side effect, had made possible the manufacture of weapons capable of greater destruction than ever before.

This small start toward a universal disarmament agreement, however, was abruptly halted by World War I, which began in 1914 and introduced to the world a whole new family of weaponry—tanks, submarines, aircraft, poison gas, and so on.

The great toll in human life and property taken by World War I triggered further efforts to halt the escalation of new and dangerous weapons. A League of Nations, somewhat similar to the present United Nations, was formed immediately after the war ended. One of its first declarations was, "The maintenance of peace requires the reduction of national armaments to the lowest point consistent with national security."

At the peace conference of Versailles, in France, the allied nations "demilitarized" Germany and imposed drastic limitations on that country's armament. The Allies also held a series of postwar negotiations, seeking to agree on restricting certain weapons.

In 1922, the Allies agreed to place certain limitations on the deployment of naval warships, and to put a freeze on naval fortifications and bases in the western Pacific Ocean area.

There was also a special emphasis placed on finding ways to ban the use of poison gases, which had killed or permanently injured thousands of soldiers during the war. In 1925, an agreement was signed at Geneva, Switzerland, prohibiting the use of poison gas and germ warfare.

There was a continued attempt to reach some agreement on general disarmament in the years between Word Wars I and II, but all efforts failed with Adolf Hitler's rise to power in Germany. Eventually, the League of Nations was dissolved.

The use of atomic bombs toward the end of World War II created a new disarmament initiative, with particular attention to stopping the spread of the terrifying new nuclear weapons. The stupendous power of these new bombs shattered all previous concepts of war and weaponry.

As the years passed, the development and spread of new technology brought additional dangers and complications. In 1949 the Soviet Union exploded its first atomic bomb. Three years later the United States detonated its first hydrogen bomb. And in 1953, this was followed by the explosion of a Russian hydrogen bomb.

These weapons had a destructive power far greater than the earlier atomic bombs. National leaders now recognized that such weapons had the potential capability to destroy a good part of the earth. The increasing strength and sophistication of such systems demanded renewed efforts at finding a solution to the increasingly complex disarmament problem.

The UN created a Disarmament Commission and other committees during the 1950s to address the problem. These later evolved into the Conference of the Committee on Disarment (CCD). In 1961 the U.S. government established a separate agency to deal with the arms race—the first national government to do so.

The U.S. Arms Control and Disarmament Agency (ACDA) is charged with developing, coordinating, and carrying out arms control policies, conducting and coordinating research, and disseminating information to the public about arms control.

Although the issue of arms control has been heatedly debated throughout the years of the nuclear age, and no fully acceptable or all-encompassing solutions have yet been found that will eliminate the threat of nuclear war or put an end to the arms race, a number of significant steps toward worldwide disarmament have been taken. Here now is a brief summary of these actions, with the exception of the SALT talks, which are discussed separately in the chapters following.

The Antarctic Treaty

The Antarctic Treaty was the earliest of the arms limitation agreements reached following the end of World War II. A number of nations had claimed certain sections of the frozen continent at the bottom of the earth, but these claims were not recognized internationally. There were also several major expeditions to Antarctica in the 1950s, but they were all scientific ventures rather than political, economic, or military ones.

Many nations had informally expressed a wish to keep the continent a neutral zone free of weapons of any kind. Consequently, the United States in 1959 invited twelve nations, which had all participated in a joint scientific venture in Antarctica in the previous two years, to a conference in Washington to set up a treaty concerning this immense, barren territory.

The ensuing agreement went into effect on June 23, 1961. It provides that Antarctica shall be used for peaceful purposes only. It specifically prohibits any "measures of a military nature, such as the establishment of military bases and fortifications, the carrying out of military maneuvers, as well as the testing of any types of weapons." Nuclear explosions and the disposal of radioactive wastes in the area are also forbidden.

Further, it was agreed that all treaty-signing nations would have free access at any time to all parts of the continent. And they can send observers at any time to inspect any installations, to make sure they are not being used for military purposes.

The treaty has worked satisfactorily through the years. One reason, experts feel, is that it is much easier to exclude armaments than it is to eliminate or control them once they have been introduced into an area.

The "Hot Line"

As the two superpowers, the United States and the Soviet Union, continued to develop, build, and refine their nuclear arsenals through the 1950s, a gnawing fear began to be felt not only by these two countries but by most of the nations of the world. What would happen if one nation accidentally, through a miscalculation, say, or a faulty computer, launched a nuclear bomb at the other? What if the whole thing was a mistake? After all, human beings do make errors. There was a great danger that the power under attack, not realizing it was an accident, would respond by launching an all-out retaliatory strike, thus starting a nuclear war.

The need for protection against such a mishap became especially clear during the Cuban Missile Crisis of October 1962. The United States had demanded that the Soviets dismantle and remove all missiles and launchers that were being constructed in Cuba. To assure that no new supplies or equipment reached the island, the United States set up a naval blockade to keep out Soviet ships then approaching Cuba. It was an exceptionally tense few days; both nations brought their military manpower and weapons up to an emergency state of readiness. In such an emotionally charged situation it became easy to see how an accident could set off a full-scale war that no one wanted.

Fortunately, both the United States and the Soviet Union recognized the danger and wished to avert it. Hence, on June 20, 1963, both nations agreed to set up direct communication links between the two countries' capitals—Washington, D.C., and Moscow. In effect, this "hot line" could be used by the president of the United States to quickly reach the head of the Soviet Union at any time and vice versa. That way, one nation could warn the other if an accident had occurred and explain what had happened and why, thus greatly reducing the risk of war.

A chilling incident that happened in 1980 is a good example of the need for such a direct communications line. Because of a computer failure, a U.S. defense system installation indicated that the Soviets had launched an ICBM toward this country, when, in fact, they had not. For a few minutes things became hectic as military personnel began alert countdowns for a possible retaliatory strike. Fortunately, a double check of the computer reporting the launch showed that it was a mechanical failure and not the real thing.

Had the computer failure not been detected in time, however, the hot line would probably have been used to call the Soviets, to try to determine whether the world was indeed in a state of war.

The Test Ban Treaty

During the 1950s, first the United States and the Soviet Union, and then other nations, set off a number of nuclear explosions in a continuing series of tests to further develop their weapon stockpiles. It seemed that each succeeding blast was larger and more powerful than the one before it.

These tests produced worldwide complaints about the contamination of the environment by radioactive substances. Indeed, the fears concerning the immediate and long-term effects of atmospheric testing of nuclear weapons were well founded. In March 1954, for example, the United States exploded an experimental thermonuclear device in the South Pacific Ocean. It was expected to have the power of 8 million tons of TNT, but the actual blast yield was almost double what had been predicted—the equivalent of 15 million tons of TNT, or 15 megatons—and the area of dangerous radioactive fallout went far beyond original estimates.

As a direct result, a Japanese fishing vessel was accidentally contaminated, and its crew suffered from radiation sickness, as did the inhabitants of an atoll in the area. In another test explosion, radioactive "rain" containing debris from a Soviet hydrogen test bomb fell on Japan.

As world protest mounted, the nuclear powers, through the UN's Disarmament Commission, in 1955 began negotiations on a new treaty to limit nuclear testing. Because there were many complicated issues involved, such as how one nation could verify that another was not secretly testing, it took eight years to reach an agreement.

Then finally, in October 1963, the treaty was signed and ratified by the United States, the Soviet Union, and the

United Kingdom. It said in part that those countries would undertake "not to carry out any nuclear weapon test explosion, or any other nuclear explosion, in the atmosphere, underwater, or in outer space—or in any other environment if the explosion would cause radioactive debris to extend beyond the borders of the state conducting the explosion."

This still left the nuclear powers free to hold bomb tests underground, but it was a big step in helping to preserve the earth's ecology from deadly radioactive fallout, which spreads out over wide areas when released into the atmosphere.

In the years since, the three original treaty-signing countries have stuck by their agreement, and 113 others have either signed or ratified the treaty. France and the People's Republic of China, which had not signed it, subsequently tested nuclear weapons in the atmosphere and underwater. India followed suit in 1974 with its explosion of a nuclear device.

The Outer Space Treaty

When Russia launched its *Sputnik* satellite into earth orbit in October 1957, it opened the Space Age. Even before that historic occasion, however, the United States and other nations had foreseen the potential dangers of using outer space for military purposes and had begun proposing ways to curb it. The Soviet Union did not participate in these early discussions, but a dialogue was nevertheless begun.

In 1960, President Dwight D. Eisenhower, speaking at the UN General Assembly, suggested that everyone treat outer space according to the same principles that had been applied to Antarctica, the idea being that since there were no weapons yet in space, it would be easier to reach a peaceful agreement. The Soviets, too, seemed ready to come to terms. But again, negotiations were slow, and many snags had to be worked out.

The Outer Space Treaty was officially agreed upon by all in October 1967, ten years after the launching of *Sputnik*. It has two important provisions. First, it declares that nations are "not to place in orbit around the earth, install on the moon or any other celestial body, or otherwise station in outer space, nuclear or any other weapons of mass destruction."

Second, it "limits the use of the moon and other celestial bodies exclusively to peaceful purposes and expressly prohibits their use for establishing military bases, installations or fortifications; testing weapons of any kind; or conducting military maneuvers."

In the years since this treaty came into force, space exploration has often been accomplished in a cooperative spirit between nations. However, in the past few years there has been evidence that the Soviet Union is building a capability to destroy satellites placed in earth orbit by other nations.

Some satellites are used in military roles such as early warning, reconnaissance, communications, and navigation. Other satellites are used in civilian activities, including meteorology, civilian communications, and scientific exploration. Photo reconnaisance satellites are used to verify that nations are following arms control agreements.

If one superpower develops a satellite-killing system, as the United States suspects the Soviet Union is, it is likely that the other superpower will try to do likewise. Since this would tend to increase instead of lessen world tension, the United States and the Soviet Union met in June 1978 to discuss ways to cope with this problem. Their aim was to come to an agreement that would prohibit attacks on satellites and to place limits on the testing and use of any system designed for attacking satellites.

To date, several meetings have been held, and some progress has been made toward an anti-satellite treaty. But still more work must be done before final agreement can be reached.

Neither superpower wishes to let the other gain sole control of space. Such domination could conceivably result in one nation's holding the rest of the world hostage. The launching of weapons from a vantage point in space would be difficult to detect and almost impossible to defend against.

The Latin American Nuclear-Free Zone

Before the Cuban Missile Crisis arose in October 1962, proposals had been made in the United States to declare Latin America a nuclear-free zone, in the same manner as Antarctica. Cuba, however, had balked at the initial treaty and had added a number of conditions that the United States would not agree to.

When the Cuban Missile Crisis occurred, though, it awoke many of the Latin American countries to the real danger of a nuclear war. In 1963, five countries—Bolivia, Brazil, Chile, Equador, and Mexico—announced that they were ready to sign a treaty. Negotiations began at the United Nations. A long series of talks among Latin American nations followed, resulting in a treaty they all could live by. It was signed at Tlatelolco, D.F., Mexico, on February 11, 1967, and became official on April 22, 1968. Cuba refused to take part.

The agreement stated that the Latin American nations would use nuclear materials and facilities exclusively for peaceful purposes. They would not, "by any means whatsoever" test, use, manufacture, produce, or acquire any nuclear weapons. And they would not receive, store, install, deploy, or possess in any form any nuclear weapons, directly or indirectly, by themselves, by anyone on their behalf, or in any other way.

Four of the world's nuclear powers, the United States, the United Kingdom, France, and China, also came to an agreement regarding the Latin American Nuclear-Free Zone. They said they would

- Respect the de-nuclearized status of the zone.
- Not contribute to acts involving violation of the treaty by nations that had ratified it.
- Not use or threaten to use nuclear weapons against any of the Latin American nations that had ratified the treaty.

The Soviet Union did not join in this agreement initially, but in 1978 it changed its position to one of accord. The United States was pleased with the treaty because it assured that there would be no future buildup of nuclear arms in Latin America such as there had been in Cuba in the early 1960s.

The Seabed Arms Control Treaty

In the 1960s, advances in oceanographic technology, and increased interest in the rich, untapped resources of the ocean floor, caused great concern among many nations of the world. There were no international rules of law covering this vast area, and there was fear that the seabed could be used as a new environment for military installations, including those capable of launching nuclear weapons.

The UN General Assembly appointed a committee in 1967 to study ways of preserving the seabed for peaceful purposes "for the benefit of all mankind."

In March 1969, President Richard M. Nixon said in an address that "discussion of the factors necessary for an international agreement prohibiting the emplacement of weapons of mass destruction on the seabed and ocean floor" should be undertaken. He said that an agreement of this kind would, like the Antarctic and Outer Space treaties, "prevent an arms race before it has a chance to start."

At the same time, the Soviet Union presented a draft treaty calling for complete demilitarization of the seabed beyond a 12-mile limit. With both superpowers obviously in favor of an agreement, the outlook was bright. Still, the United States and the Soviet Union had some differing views on specific points in the treaty, and it took two years to straighten them out. The pact was signed on February 11, 1971, and was ratified and came into force on May 18, 1972.

Under Article I of the agreement, nations are prohibited from emplacing nuclear weapons or other weapons of mass destruction on the seabed and the ocean floor beyond a 12-mile coastal zone. The United States, the United Kingdom, the Soviet Union, and more than twenty other nations initially ratified the treaty.

Reducing the Risk of Accidental Nuclear War

During some preliminary disarmament discussions between the United States and the Soviet Union in the early 1970s, it became apparent that both sides were deeply concerned about the growing possibility of nuclear war being started by accident. The two countries realized that despite the hot line and the most careful precautions, any number of incidents could conceivably "pull the trigger," including a technical failure, a human error, a misunderstood action, or an action taken without the approval of U.S. or Soviet leaders.

To help prevent any such accidental occurrence, the United States and the Soviet Union, on September 30, 1971, signed an Agreement on Measures to Reduce the Risk of Outbreak of Nuclear War Between the United States of America and the Union of Soviet Socialist Republics. Basically, this agreement did three things:

■ Both sides pledged to maintain and improve the safeguards against accidental or unauthorized use of nuclear weapons.

■ Arrangements would be made so that one country could immediately contact the other should an accidental use of nuclear weapons occur, should unidentified objects be picked up on early warning systems, or should a nuclear weapon be accidentally detonated.

■ Both sides agreed that advance warning would be made of any planned missile launches beyond the territory of the launching nation and in the direction of the other nation.

On the same date that this agreement was signed, the United States and the Soviet Union also agreed to modernize their hot-line communications system by establishing satellite communications circuits between the two countries.

Biological Weapons Convention

The extensive use of poison gas in World War I resulted in over a million casualties and more than 100,000 deaths. This led to the international agreement made in 1925, which banned the use of both poison gas and germ warfare.

Although such weapons were not used in World War II, nations still developed and stockpiled them during and after the war. But most nations of the world were in general agreement that such hideous weapons should be outlawed.

After several years of negotiations, a pact was signed by most of the countries of the world on April 10, 1972, with participating nations agreeing "not to develop, produce, stockpile, or acquire biological agents or toxins of types and in quantities that have no justification for . . . protective, or other peaceful use." The countries also consented to destroy all such materials then in their possession within nine months.

The question of a ban on chemical warfare is more complex and is still being discussed. While most nations seem to have lived up to the poison gas and biological warfare agreements, a number of these same nations, including the United States and the Soviet Union, have continued to develop chemical-weapons technology and to use it to build large arsenals of such weapons.

The goal of the United Nations is to reach an agreement that will lead to prohibiting the development, production, and stockpiling of chemical weapons. Serious talks have been held since 1971, and U.S. and Soviet representatives have met a number of times to iron out differences. There is reason to hope that these differences will be resolved in the near future.

Limitation of Underground Nuclear Weapons Tests

Following the limited test ban treaty of 1963 and the non-proliferation treaty of 1968, both the United States and the Soviet Union expressed their hope of eventually discontinuing all nuclear weapons tests, including underground explosions.

Working toward this goal, these two countries signed an agreement on July 3, 1974, under which

■ Each nation agreed not to carry out any tests of weapons having a yield in excess of 150 kilotons after March 31, 1976.
■ Each nation promised to keep its underground tests to a minimum, and to work toward ending all underground nuclear weapons tests.

Indian Ocean Zone of Peace

For centuries, the Indian Ocean and the regions surrounding it have been of strategic military importance. In the nuclear weapons age this is still true. In light of this fact, serious efforts began in the early 1970s to declare the Indian Ocean area a zone of peace, much as Latin America is a nuclear-free zone.

While this aim has not been accomplished despite nearly a decade of work and negotiations by the United Nations and others, some progress has been made, and it is highly possible that a zone of peace may be declared and agreed to by all nations in the near future.

8

SALT I

Although a number of arms control treaties and agreements have been reached over the past two decades, the issue of major importance—halting the escalation of nuclear weapons building by the United States and the Soviet Union—remains unresolved. These two nations have continued to spend billions of dollars strengthening their military systems.

Attempts at getting these two nuclear powers together to seek some way of stopping or slowing the arms race have been made for many years, dating back to the time when they both first displayed the ability to build and explode atomic bombs. But it was not until November 1969 that such negotiations seriously began. These first sessions were called the Strategic Arms Limitation Talks, or SALT I. They were continuing discussions between the United States and the Soviet Union on the subject of limiting and reducing strategic nuclear weapons.

At the very beginning of these talks, the United States spelled out some specific objectives that would have to be met to insure its security and that of its allies; otherwise little or no progress could be made. These objectives included the following:

■ Any agreement must leave the United States and its allies at least as strong in relation to the Soviet Union as they would be without such an agreement.

■ The agreement must insure that the Soviets not obtain an advantage in strategic forces.

■ It must also permit the United States the flexibility to respond to any new Soviet challenges or threats not covered by the talks.

One of the initial goals of SALT was to maintain the stability or balance of power that exists between the two greatest nuclear nations. It was recognized that should one nation develop new and more powerful weapons that could threaten the other side, the delicate balance could be upset. One of SALT's objectives, then, would be to see that this didn't happen.

It was hoped, too, that the SALT negotiations would help lay the foundation for an improved overall relationship between the United States and the Soviet Union.

When the SALT I talks were first announced, they were hailed as a major breakthrough. Some people expected instant results. But in a published bulletin the U.S. State Department warned against such optimism: "There have been many unrealistic expectations for SALT. It has sometimes been seen as a way of sharply reducing defense spending, or as a means by which all threats against U.S. forces could be eliminated. Some have hoped that SALT would usher in a new era of U.S./Soviet cooperation and do away with military rivalry across the board."

The bulletin pointed out that while such hopes were understandable, they were not likely to be quickly realized. "Neither side is ready at this point for far-reaching disarmament schemes. SALT agreements, while they can reduce strategic forces on both sides and restrict the introduction of new strategic weapons, cannot substitute for prudent U.S. efforts to maintain forces which meet our strategic objectives."

The State Department said, in so many words, that people should not expect an agreement that would immediately put an end to the nuclear arms race. Rather, it said, the choice facing the United States was between a good agreement protecting and enhancing national security and no agreement at all.

It was against this background and general understanding that the SALT I talks officially began in Helsinki, Finland, on November 17, 1969. The two nations met, off and on, for a period of two and a half years, seeking agreements to place limits and restraints on some of the "central and most important armaments."

One key area of discussion was antiballistic missile (ABM) systems. As a defense against incoming nuclear warheads launched from missiles, the Soviet Union, in 1966, began to build an ABM system around Moscow, its capital city. This system included a network of launchers and missiles designed to knock out incoming missiles before they could reach their targets. A year later, following intense pressure from the public and Congress, the United States announced it would build its own limited ABM system.

Such a system was feasible, and the technology to produce it was available. The problem was cost. An ABM system to adequately protect both missile sites and urban population areas would cost tens of billions of dollars. And by the time such a system could be set up, new developments in offensive nuclear weapons might render ABMs out of date within a short period of time. It would take billions of dollars more to keep such a system up to date.

Recognizing that this was folly, the United States and the Soviet Union decided it would be best for both nations to come to an agreement limiting the number of ABM sites and systems. It was also felt that such an agreement could not only end increasing competition in defensive systems but at the same time eliminate the need to build the even more powerful offensive weapons that would be required to penetrate ABM-guarded sites.

In 1972, the ABM treaty was signed and put into effect. It limited each side to two sites that could be protected. At each site there would be no more than a hundred interceptor missiles and a hundred launchers. In 1974, the two nations refined this agreement and cut back the number of ABM sites allowable to one. This one site can be used to protect the capital of a country or one of its nuclear weapons bases. Through this treaty, each nation leaves itself open to massive retalitatory nuclear attack should it initiate such an attack.

The decision to restrict the number of ABM sites relieved both countries of an enormous economic burden that would have strained national budgets for a long time.

Additionally, during the SALT I talks, the United States and the Soviet Union sought ways to come to an agreement on limitations of strategic offensive nuclear weapons. This issue was far more complex and difficult, however, and progress was much slower.

Finally, in 1972, the two countries reached an interim agreement on "certain measures with respect to the limitation of strategic offensive arms." This temporary pact essentially put a freeze on the current total number of strategic ICBM launchers and submarine launchers, either already in use or under construction.

The United States had 1,054 land-based ICBMs in place and none under construction. The Soviet Union had an estimated 1,618 ICBMs operational or under construction. The two countries agreed not to start construction of any additional ICBM launchers during the period of the interim treaty. They would also not relocate existing launchers, or convert light or older ICBM launchers into launchers for modern heavy ICBMs.

Mobile ICBM systems were not included in the restrictions. With respect to submarine-launched ballistic missile systems, the United States, under the interim agreement, is permitted to reach a ceiling of 710 launchers on 44 submarines. This is an increase from its base level of 656 SLBM launchers on 41 ballistic missile submarines. The Soviet Union is permitted to raise its number of SLBMs to 950—up from a base level of 740. But these additional launchers are allowed only as replacements for older ICBM or SLBM launchers, which must then be dismantled or destroyed.

The first round of SALT talks was climaxed on May 26, 1972, when President Richard M. Nixon and Soviet Communist party General Secretary Leonid I. Brezhnev signed both the ABM treaty and the interim agreement on strategic offensive arms.

There was a lot of disappointment in the United States, in the Soviet Union, and in other nations around the world that the agreements had not gone further. For example, no positive steps had been taken toward cutting back the lethal nuclear arsenals each country still possessed.

The nuclear submarine *USS Ohio* undergoing sea trials in 1981.

9

SALT II: AN OVERVIEW

Six months after the SALT I treaty was ratified, discussion began between the United States and the Soviet Union on a more comprehensive SALT II agreement. Among the key issues were finding a means to establish equality in strategic nuclear forces and placing specific limits on the numbers of nuclear weapons that would be allowed each country.

While the intentions were good, the results of these early negotiations were not. There were many points on which the two countries could not agree, and very little progress was made over the next two years.

In November 1974, however, President Gerald R. Ford met with Soviet leader Brezhnev in Vladivostok, and a major opening in the deadlocked talks was achieved. Ford and Brezhnev came to terms on basic guidelines for a SALT II agreement, including a ceiling on the total number of strategic nuclear "delivery vehicles" (ICBM launchers, SLBM launchers, and heavy bombers) each country could maintain and a limit on the total number of MIRV systems. Construction of new fixed ICBM launchers and conversion of older fixed launchers from light to heavy ICBMs were banned.

Limits were placed on putting into a state of readiness any new types of strategic offensive arms, and strict measures to verify that both sides were following the rules were to be added to the treaty. It was also agreed that theater nuclear forces, such as the U.S.-NATO forces in Europe, would not be counted in the allowable totals. The SALT II treaty was to be in effect through 1985.

Although the major points had been approved by both sides, the negotiations again became bogged down, this time over the details. Two issues in particular caused trouble. One was how to classify cruise missiles. Should they be included in the total of strategic nuclear weapons? The other issue concerned the Soviet Backfire bomber aircraft. Should it be classified as a heavy bomber and therefore be subject to the total count, or should it be excluded?

The talks continued. Finally, in 1977, it was agreed that the cruise missile and Backfire questions would be set aside temporarily for solution at a later date. Another problem, what to do about mobile ICBM launchers, was also held off for further consideration later.

On June 18, 1979, President Jimmy Carter and Leonid Brezhnev signed the SALT II Treaty at a summit meeting in Vienna, Austria, following more than six and a half years of talks.

Here are the major points covered in the treaty:

■ The United States and the Soviet Union would limit the total number of strategic nuclear delivery vehicles to 2,400 each. This number would be further reduced to 2,250 in 1981.
■ Each side would limit the total number of launchers of MIRVed ballistic missiles and heavy bombers equipped for long-range cruise missiles to 1,320.
■ The number of launchers of MIRVed ballistic missiles was set at 1,200, and a limit of 820 was placed on launchers of MIRVed ICBMs.
■ No new fixed ICBM launchers would be built.
■ A ban was placed on the flight-testing and use of new types of ICBMs, with the exception of one new type of ICBM.

**U.S. President Jimmy Carter and
Soviet President Leonid Brezhnev
sign the SALT II agreement
on June 18, 1979.**

- The number of warheads on existing types of ICBMs could not be increased. Up to ten warheads could be added to the one new type of ICBM. Limits of fourteen warheads were assigned to SLBMs and ten warheads to air-to-surface ballistic missiles (those launched from bombers).
- Ceilings were placed on the launch weight and throw weight (the power of launchers) of strategic ballistic missiles.
- A ban was placed on the production, testing, and deployment of the Soviet SS-16 missile.
- A ban was placed on rapid reload ICBM systems (systems that allow more than one ICBM to be fired from the same launcher over a short span of time).
- A ban was placed on certain types of nuclear offensive weapons that were technically possible to develop but that had not yet been built, such as long-range ballistic missiles on surface ships, ballistic missile launchers on the seabed, fractional orbital bombardment systems (which could be launched into earth orbit and reenter the atmosphere at a distant point), and mobile launchers of heavy ICBMs or heavy SLBMs.
- An alert system would be set up to give advance warning of simultaneous multiple ICBM test launches (so as not to trigger an accidental retaliatory strike).

Additionally, the two sides agreed to ban the deployment of mobile ICBM launchers and the flight-testing of ICBMs from such launchers. This addition, however, was to last only through 1981, after which deployment of mobile ICBM launchers would be permitted.

The ban on cruise missiles capable of ranges in excess of 600 kilometers on ground-based and sea-based launchers was also to be in effect only through 1981. Further, the treaty included a ban on flight-testing and deployment of air-to-surface ballistic missiles through 1981.

Another SALT II element established a framework for the next stage of the SALT talks—SALT III—to begin at some point in the future. The United States and the Soviet Union agreed that in those talks the primary goals should be further reductions in the number of strategic offensive arms on both sides and further "qualitative limitations" on these arms (such as the number of warheads permitted on missiles, the replacement of older systems with newer and more advanced ones, and so on).

One of the single most important considerations of the entire SALT process is verification. This is the means by which each country can check and make sure the other is doing all it promised it would do under the treaty. Without such verification, one country could conceivably "cheat," by continuing to build weapons over and above the agreed-upon limits and could thus gain a weapons superiority over the other.

Both the United States and the Soviet Union believe they have the technology to assure verification. Speaking of this issue in 1979, President Carter said, "Our confidence in the verifiability of the [SALT II] agreement derives from the size and nature of activities we must monitor and the many effective and sophisticated intelligence collection systems which we in America possess."

"For example," the president said, "nuclear submarines take several years to construct and assemble. Missile silos and their supportive equipment are quite large and visible. Intercontinental bombers are built at a few plants, and they need major airfields. Our photo reconnaissance satellites survey the entire Soviet Union on a regular basis."

Indeed, these high-technology satellites have the capability of sighting and photographing even small objects from a distance of a hundred miles or more above the earth. U.S. ships and aircraft also continually monitor Soviet missile tests, and ground stations such as the large U.S. radar facility on Shemya Island in Alaska gather data on such tests.

Both sides agreed not to hinder the verification process in any way and not to conceal activities of their strategic forces.

"As I have said many times," President Carter added, "the stakes are too high to rely on trust, or even on the Soviets' rational inclination to act in their own best interest. The treaty must—and the treaty will be—verifiable from the first day it is signed."

As mentioned earlier, the SALT II treaty was signed in 1979 by the president of the United States and by the Soviet leader. But before it could officially become a binding agreement, it would have to be ratified by the U.S. Senate.

Despite the strong efforts of President Jimmy Carter and Defense Secretary Harold Brown, the treaty failed to win ratification in the Senate before the Carter administration ended in January 1981. From the moment SALT II was submitted to the Senate, it encountered sharp opposition from many members. The senators questioned the overall fairness of the treaty, saying that it called for the United States to give up too much in comparison to what the Russians would have to give up. They felt it contained too many loopholes that the Soviets would make use of to continue their nuclear arms buildup. They also contended that the treaty did not go far enough in limiting and dismantling nuclear weapons, and said that SALT II would lead to a weakening of the U.S. defense position and create an imbalance between the two leading nuclear powers.

In December 1979, the Soviet Union invaded the country of Afghanistan. This aggressive action made the American public suspicious of true Soviet intentions in regard to world peace and disarmament. There was a general outcry in the United States against signing the SALT II treaty until the Soviets removed their troops from Afghanistan.

The chances for ratification of SALT II, slim as they were at this point, disappeared almost completely with the election of Ronald Reagan as president of the United States in November 1980.

Reagan had made SALT II one of his main campaign issues. He was flatly against it. "First of all, it permits a continued arms buildup on both sides," he said at a press conference in January 1981, shortly after he took office. "It allows an immediate increase of Soviet warheads and no limits. How can strategic arms limitation talks allow a continued buildup? We should start negotiations on the basis of actually reducing arms. That's a real SALT."

Let's take a closer look now at specific objections made to the treaty when it was before the Senate for ratification.

10

SALT II:
THE CASE AGAINST

Millions of Americans—no one knows exactly how many millions—are opposed to the SALT talks altogether, or to any form of arms limitation negotiations. Instead, they feel that the United States must build up its military strength to the point where it is again the superior power in the world, and it must maintain this position. Anything less, they fear, will eventually lead to a Communist takeover.

Most of these people are political conservatives, and many of their leaders are Evangelical ministers who have built up large followings in recent years through their own television programs. This segment of the population seems to have a special fear of the Soviet Union and its intentions in the world.

"The Soviets have always had one goal, and that is to destroy capitalistic society. They are a nation committed to communism and to destroying the American way of life," declares the Reverend Jerry Falwell, a nationally known Evangelist who is the head of a large conservative political lobbying organization called the Moral Majority. This organization took an active part in the 1980 presidential and congressional campaigns and claims its efforts helped many conservative Republican candidates to get elected.

"Communists know that in order to take over a country they must first see to it that a nation's military strength is weakened and that its morals are corrupted so that its people have no will to resist wrong," Falwell says. "Our enemies know that when we are weak morally, and when we have lost our will to fight, we are in a precarious position for takeover. The Soviets are liars and cheaters. They are determined to conquer our free country and to infiltrate the American people with godless communism."

James Robison, of Fort Worth, Texas, another popular television preacher whose audiences number in the millions, says: "As a minister, I've been asked several times how defense can be a moral issue. I believe that it is very definitely a moral issue. We have a global menace today [the Soviet Union] who terrorizes the entire world. If we as a people refuse to have the defense capability to corral and control a menace that has threatened the freedom of the entire world, I believe we as a people have become immoral."

Terry Dolan, head of the National Conservative Political Action Committee, adds: "We often are asked how you can arm and be peaceful at the same time. In fact, the best way to be peaceful is to be armed. George Washington said that. The best way to stay free is to be strong. The American people are sick and tired of being number two."

Consequently, this group was incensed by government decisions during the Carter administration that resulted in the cancellation of the B-1 strategic bomber program, the delay of the MX mobile intercontinental ballistic missile system, and various other military cutbacks.

"By militarily disarming our country," Falwell charges, "we have actually been surrendering our rights and our sovereignty, and as the Soviets would soon like to see—our freedoms and other liberties. It is only common sense that disarmament is suicide. We need leaders of moral courage today who know that there is safety in strength not in weakness."

Having a strong national defense became one of the key issues of the 1980 election campaign. Many experts think that Ronald Reagan's hard-line pro-defense stand helped him to win the election over Jimmy Carter. It also seems to have played a major role in congressional elections. Many senators, for example, who were portrayed by their opponents as weak on defense lost in the elections.

Falwell and other politically conservative leaders, and the millions of Americans who subscribe to their beliefs, were particularly opposed to the SALT II disarmament treaty. They felt it would have unfairly hampered the U.S. military buildup while allowing the Soviet Union to continue building and stockpiling superior weapons systems.

Others who were opposed to the SALT II treaty said they were not against arms control per se. But they strongly believed that SALT II was not fair and equitable to both sides and that it should be discarded in favor of negotiations for a new, better-balanced treaty.

Senator Henry M. Jackson of the state of Washington summed up his misgivings about the treaty as follows:

> Like so many others, I was disappointed at the outcome of the SALT II negotiations. What is required for the peace of the world is serious East-West arms reduction—a genuine stabilizing arms limitation. Tragically, the SALT II treaty submitted to the Senate turned out to be an unbalanced charter sanctioning the massive buildup of Soviet strategic power, advantaging the Soviets in critical respects, and containing provisions of great importance that we are unable to verify.
>
> If the United States settled for an unequal SALT II agreement, what is going to persuade Moscow to accept an "equal" agreement in a SALT III or a SALT IV? The free nations will be far better off if the Senate insists on equality now, in SALT II, rather than hope that the next time around equality will be achieved.
>
> Just remember that SALT II was to have been the "next time" as a follow-up to SALT I. It is now generally

recognized that the SALT agreement of 1972 did not, as its proponents hoped, moderate the growth of Soviet strategic forces. In fact, Soviet spending on strategic forces actually increased after the 1972 agreement.

Added Senator Jesse Helms of North Carolina: "The Soviets have used . . . the SALT process to obtain superior power. They have realized they could never compete with us in an all-out arms race. They therefore used the SALT process as a shield for the construction of nuclear arms. The vast majority of the Soviet nuclear arms which are aimed at us today were built and deployed during the SALT process. Far from limiting strategic arms, the SALT process has been a technique for a quantum leap in Soviet arms construction."

In December 1979, the Senate Armed Services Committee, after hearing testimony from dozens of expert witnesses and reading through thousands of pages of documents and testimony pertaining to SALT over a period of several months, issued a report highly critical of the treaty. The committee went on record with its judgment that the treaty "as it now stands, is not in the national security interests of the United States."

In summarizing its analysis of the treaty and of the current and future world situation, the committee said that for the first time in the history of the nuclear age, the United States now faced "a near certainty that a significant element of its strategic deterrent [force] will be vulnerable" to destruction on a first strike attack by the Soviet Union.

The committee added that it was faced with overwhelming evidence that even with SALT II, by the 1980s the Soviet Union would have the capacity to destroy virtually the entire U.S. land-based missile force. It said that the United States did not and would not have a similar capability to destroy Soviet ICBM forces. It said that, though the United States still retained an awesome strategic nuclear power, it was highly questionable how much damage could be done to the Soviet land-based ICBM arsenal in a retaliatory strike. This finding was based on the following points:

■ U.S. bombing capability is based on an "aging fleet of B-52 aircraft built, on the average, some twenty-five years ago and unlikely to be effective in timely retaliation against hardened/defended military targets—even with the addition of cruise missiles."

■ "The U.S. fleet of strategic nuclear submarines . . . carries missiles that lack the combination of accuracy and yield necessary to destroy hardened military targets."

■ The U.S. land-based ICBMs would be ineffective in a retaliatory strike because if the Russians struck first, they could knock out up to 95 percent of this force.

Thus, the committee concluded that ratification of SALT II would be in violation of public law 92–448, which Congress enacted in the early 1970s, just as the first SALT II talks were getting under way. This law states: "The Congress urges and requests the President to seek a future treaty that would not limit the United States to levels of intercontinental strategic forces inferior to the limits provided for the Soviet Union."

Here, now, is a summary of the major arguments that have been raised against SALT II:

1. It would lock the United States into strategic inferiority, because the treaty does not provide for equal numbers of weapons or equality in overall strategic power. Several Soviet strategic weapons were not included in SALT II—principally the Backfire bomber and the new mobile intermediate-range ballistic missile, which could quickly be converted into an ICBM that could strike the United States. Both of these weapons are being produced by the Soviets in large numbers.

The Backfire was excluded from the SALT II treaty because it was classified as a tactical, or theater, weapon that would be based in the Soviet Union and did not have the range to reach the United States. SALT II opponents, however, say it has a range of 6,500 miles (10,500 km) and could be refueled in flight, thus giving it the potential capability of being used as a strategic nuclear bomber against the United States.

In addition, the treaty would grant the Soviet Union the right to have over 300 "heavy" ICBMs. These are more powerful than any ICBMs the United States plans to have and can carry up to ten nuclear warheads each, whereas U.S. ICBMs can carry only three. Each warhead is rated at just over one megaton.

These heavy Soviet ICBMs are six times more powerful than the U.S. Minuteman ICBMs. In fact, the destructive power of the Soviet SS-18 ICBMs alone, if each were armed with ten warheads, would be greater than that of all the U.S. ICBMs and SLBMs combined.

According to intelligence estimates, the Soviets will have their entire force of heavy ICBMs in place, aimed at the United States, by the early 1980s. They will have the capability, with their 3,000 warheads, of destroying up to 95 percent of the U.S. ICBM force, with enough warheads left over for attacks on bomber and submarine bases.

Also, after a first strike, the Soviets would be left with more missiles and bombers for a second strike than the United States had to start with. Some experts contended that if the United States counterattacked after a first strike, the Soviets could aim bombers and missiles at cities, kill 100 million Americans, and destroy the United States as a society.

2. SALT II would make a hostage of America. Because of agreements reached in the SALT I treaty, the United States does not have an adequate defense system to protect nuclear weapons sites, industrial centers, or the general population. This is because the United States has followed a policy called Mutual Assured Destruction (MAD). The theory is that neither nuclear power would launch a first strike for fear of being attacked in return.

**A Titan II missile launch
from an underground silo at
Vandenberg Air Force Base
in California.**

However, SALT II opponents contended that modern ICBMs are now so accurate that a massive advantage goes to the side striking the first blow. A good part of the retaliatory strike force would be destroyed before it could be launched. Further, the Soviets have developed extensive air defense and civil defense programs to lessen their losses from a retaliatory attack. All of this, treaty opponents said, has weakened U.S. strategic defenses, increased the Soviet strategic advantage, and put the American people in the position of being potential hostages to Soviet nuclear blackmail.

3. It was the opinion of those who opposed SALT II that the treaty could not be verified to assure the United States that the Soviet Union was living up to the terms of the agreement. They said that U.S. reconnaissance satellites could not determine the number of warheads on ballistic missiles; the range of a cruise missile; the number of cruise missiles on a ship, submarine, or aircraft; or the number of mobile missiles or other missiles hidden from view in storage.

4. Taking the argument in point one—that SALT II would lock the United States into strategic inferiority—even further, treaty opponents asserted that this would remove the American nuclear "shield" used to protect our allies, particularly NATO. The belief here was that in the past, although we had weaker conventional and theater weapons forces than the Soviet Union, we could always back them up with the threat of using our strategic nuclear forces. But if we lost equality with respect to these forces, such threats would no longer be credible.

5. Ratification of SALT II, said anti-treaty organizations, would be interpreted as a sign of U.S. weakness. These organizations believe that U.S. "toleration" of a Soviet strategic advantage would be viewed by the rest of the world as a symbol of America's loss of determination to defend itself and the free world from Soviet expansion.

6. Approval of SALT II would actually prove more expensive in defense costs than its rejection, according to treaty opponents. They pointed out that the least expensive ways to rebuild U.S. strategic strength would not be permitted under the treaty.

Anti-SALT II forces said that the one virtue of the treaty was that, during the ratification process before the Senate, it demanded a major review of the U.S. strategic posture, of the relative balance of power between the United States and the Soviet Union, and of overall U.S. defense and foreign policies.

SALT II opponents said that the review clearly showed that the balance of power had shifted and would continue to shift in favor of the Soviet Union—and that, in fact, ratification of the treaty would accelerate this trend.

They referred to a warning given by Alexander Solzhenitsyn, the exiled Russian writer now living in the United States: "There is no guarantee for anything in the West. You want to believe otherwise, so you cut down your armies, you cut down your research. But believe me, the Soviet Union is not cutting down anything. Soon they will be twice as powerful as you, and then five times, and then ten times. And someday they will say to you, 'We are marching our troops into Western Europe and if you act, we shall annihilate you.' And the troops will move, and you will not act."

In backing the rejection of SALT II, anti-treaty organizations offered a number of recommendations that they felt would better assure world peace. Among these recommendations were the following:

■ To regain overall military and technological superiority over the Soviet Union, the idea being that the Russians will never start a war they are sure to lose.

■ To build a strategic defense and a civil defense that will protect U.S. citizens against nuclear war at least as well as the Soviets protect their citizens.

■ To accept no arms control agreement that in any way jeopardizes the security of the United States or its allies, or that inhibits a superior U.S. defense.

■ To adopt a policy of helping U.S. allies and other noncommunist countries defend themselves against internal and external Communist takeover.

■ To establish superior security and intelligence capabilities.

One final point concerning many of those who opposed SALT II was expressed by Robert C. Richardson III, a retired Air Force Brigadier General who was an active member of one anti-SALT organization. "It should be made quite clear," Richardson said, "that just because some people in the United States oppose arms control agreements such as the SALT II treaty, this doesn't make them prowar arms merchants. In fact, we are advocating a road to peace which has been historically far more successful than arms control—peace through strength."

Backers of this point of view noted what the Greek historian Thucydides said nearly 2,500 years ago: "War is a bad thing; but to submit to the dictation of other states is worse. Freedom, if we hold fast to it, will ultimately restore our losses, but submission will mean permanent loss of all that we value. To you who call yourselves lovers of peace I say, you are not safe unless you have men of action at your side."

11

SALT II: THE CASE FOR

Those who had favored passage of the SALT II treaty also had strong points of argument.

"There is *no defense* against nuclear weapons," said Katherine L. Camp, president of the Women's International League for Peace and Freedom, one of many organizations that supported the treaty. "It is inconceivable for me to think one could objectively present both sides of the issue—armament and disarmament. It's like being objective about which is better, good or evil, life or death, war or peace."

"If I could have my way," said Congresswoman Patricia Schroeder of Colorado, "the world would do away with all nuclear weapons. Unfortunately, that is not a realistic possibility. Thus, I support a continuation of the SALT negotiations. The development of sound arms control agreements will give nations the opportunity, as well as the obligation, to keep searching for better ways to maintain world peace and security."

"We cannot eliminate the competition between two such dissimilar systems as the Soviet Union and the United States," said former Senator Frank Church of Idaho. "But the two countries . . . can seek to reduce the probability of nuclear war. They can strive to stabilize relations, to remove uncertainties, to eliminate incentives that spur the arms race, to open channels of communication, and to clarify the rules by which they will endeavor to live on the same planet. That is what the SALT process is all about. Perhaps it will lead us to the point where we could truly think the unthinkable— about deep reduction and eventual elimination of nuclear arms. In the meantime, we can put a ceiling on their number, hoping that this will slow down and finally stop the race toward oblivion."

Harold Brown, former U.S. secretary of defense, said: "The SALT process itself is important to the further development of U.S.-Soviet and overall East-West relations." And Zbigniew Brzezinski, former assistant to President Carter for national security affairs, said: "We have gained or retained one or more advantages for ourselves for every one we have granted the Soviet Union. And where any Soviet capability truly presents a military problem, we are free, within the terms of the agreement, to respond in appropriate ways to guarantee our security."

Townsend Hoopes and Charles Yost, executive co-chairmen of an organization called Americans for SALT, warned: "Failure to ratify SALT II would abruptly interrupt this process of controlling and reversing the arms race. It would lead inevitably to an escalation of political tensions between the United States and the Soviet Union and to sharp increases in strategic nuclear arms expenditures by both countries. An arms race thus unrestrained by any agreed limits would undermine the present strategic balance and pose grave new dangers to both countries, to their allies, and indeed to all mankind. World peace and America's security depend fundamentally on joint determination and action by the superpowers to curb the strategic arms race."

When the SALT II treaty was signed by U.S. and Soviet leaders in Vienna in June 1979, Leonid Brezhnev, the Soviet president, said, "In signing this treaty, we are helping to defend the most sacred right of every individual—the right to

"It's an absolutely fantastic weapon and deterrent.
The only trouble is it'll use up
all the rest of the money in the country."

live. To act in such a way as to prevent an outbreak of nuclear war is an obligation that the Soviet Union and the United States have jointly assumed. The treaty that has been signed today reaffirms our desire to fulfill that obligation."

To this President Carter added: "Today, the threat of nuclear holocaust still hangs over us, as it has for more than thirty years. Our two nations are now armed with thousands of nuclear weapons, each capable of causing devastation beyond measure and beyond imagination. Weapons technology has continued to advance, and so have the dangers and the obvious need to control and to regulate this arms competition.

"The Strategic Arms Limitation Talks, which have gone on for nearly ten years without interruption, represent the realization that a nuclear arms competition without shared rules and without verifiable limits and without a continuing dialogue would be an invitation to disaster."

"In our lifetime," President Carter continued, "we have learned to make war by unlocking the atom—the power of creation itself. To make peace we must limit the use of that power. . . . In setting our hands to this treaty, we set our nations on a safer course."

What were some of the specific points made by those who favor ratification of SALT II? In brief, proponents pointed out that the treaty would do the following:

■ It would place equal ceilings on the nuclear forces of the United States and the Soviet Union.
■ It would require the Soviets to dismantle 250 missile launchers and bombers—10 percent of their nuclear force. The ceiling of 2,250 on all types of strategic delivery vehicles would for the first time require the scrapping of existing weapons. Instead of allowing increases, it would at last reverse the arms race. This would make it easier to achieve more significant reductions in the future.
■ It would restrict the introduction of new types of nuclear weapons.

■ It would permit the United States to modernize its existing forces and to continue military cooperation with its allies.

■ It would ban Soviet concealment of nuclear forces or interference with American verification systems and would call for tighter controls, more verification, and stabilizing measures in SALT III.

Rejection of SALT II, said its backers, will lead to:

■ unprecedented buildups in nuclear arsenals;
■ accelerated spread of nuclear weapons to other countries;
■ higher defense budgets and more inflation;
■ a tension-charged atmosphere of conflict and confrontation; and
■ increased risk of nuclear war.

What about those arguments against SALT II, the ones discussed in the last chapter? SALT backers provided the following answers.

To the charge that SALT II would lock the United States into strategic inferiority, they said this is not true, pointing out that the secretary of defense and the chairman of the Joint Chiefs of Staff had testified before Congress that the strategic nuclear forces of the United States and the Soviet Union were essentially equal.

A report issued by Americans for SALT stated: "The United States will retain under SALT II a powerful, flexible deterrent force that can, under any circumstances, retaliate and devastate Soviet military, industrial, and—if desired—civilian targets. No possible Soviet gain from attacking our ICBMs would warrant the risk to their society of our retaliation.

"The U.S. has a very strong, balanced triad of strategic forces unsurpassed in overall capability by the Soviet Union. The Soviet forces are largely composed of fixed land-based ICBMs, which will become increasingly vulnerable in the decades ahead. Our invulnerable submarine missile forces, equipped with more than 5,000 warheads [the Soviets have about 1,000], continue to be further modernized with the Trident subs and missiles. Our 350 intercontinental bombers, a large fraction of which will soon be equipped with thousands of highly accurate cruise missiles, are vastly superior to the 150 ancient bombers of the Soviet Union. Their cruise missile technology is years behind that of the United States."

The report continued: "The Soviet SS-20 IRBM and Backfire bomber are excluded [from the treaty] because they are theater systems [do not have intercontinental range]. If any [Backfire] planes acquire a capability to launch long-range cruise missiles, they will come under ceilings [of the treaty]. It also is noted that the agreement does not restrict U.S. F-111 bombers based in Great Britain, or other aircraft which could be used against the Soviet Union."

Additionally, answering the question of Soviet superiority in heavy ICBMs, SALT proponents said that the United States has never had an interest in building such systems, preferring instead to concentrate on building high quality, reliability, and accuracy into its missiles. Furthermore, SALT II placed important restrictions on how the Soviets could use their heavy missiles, by limiting the number of warheads each could carry.

To the charge that SALT II would make our people hostages, SALT backers said that a nuclear conflict would be just as suicidal for the nation that launched a first strike as for its victim. The Americans for SALT report states: "There is no defense—military or civil—that can protect the majority of our people or those of the Soviet Union in the event of a strategic exchange between the two countries. Deterrence of a nuclear strike is the key element to security in the nuclear age, and the United States has and will maintain under SALT II a strong, effective, and flexible deterrent force."

To the charge that SALT II is unverifiable, SALT proponents said that, on the contrary, SALT II would be highly verifiable by "national technical means," which include not only photographic and electronic satellites but also many other sensors at ground stations, on ships at sea, and in aircraft.

On this point, Brzezinski added: "We maintain a vast, sophisticated array of means to detect and monitor what the Soviet Union is doing in its strategic programs. They are totally under our own control; in no way do they require us to simply trust Soviet good will. We are able to monitor many aspects of the development, testing production, deployment, training, and operation of Soviet strategic forces, despite the closed nature of Soviet society and despite Soviet obsession with secrecy."

To the charge that SALT II would remove the American nuclear shield that is used to protect our allies, pro-SALT forces said that the U.S. nuclear "umbrella" would be completely unaffected by the treaty.

Furthermore, those who favor the treaty said it actually would improve the strategic balance in favor of the United States and so could not be seen as a symbol of U.S. surrender to the Soviets. According to the Americans for SALT report: "Without SALT II, the Soviets could have 3,000 or more strategic delivery vehicles [they could have 2,250 under SALT II], more MIRVed ICBMs, more warheads, and more extensive weapons development programs." In fact, the Americans for SALT group projected that the Soviet Union would build their arsenal to "unprecedented levels," adding as many as 13,000 to 18,000 additional nuclear warheads and bombs, without SALT II.

"SALT II should be supported because it enhances our security," the report continued. "It cannot be used to extract good behavior from the Soviets around the world, and to try to do so would only risk losing the benefits it provides the United States. Arms control is more important between nations with politically different goals. It is precisely because we have such strong differences with the Soviets that we need a SALT treaty."

Finally, to the charge that ratifying SALT II would cost more than rejecting it, treaty-backers responded in the Americans for SALT report as follows: "Even with SALT II, we will spend additional defense dollars to modernize all three legs of our strategic triad. But the costs of the unrestrained arms race that would follow a rejection of SALT II would be massive compared to spending under it."

Just how high these costs would go was addressed by Congressman Les Aspin of Wisconsin. "Ratification [of the treaty] means perhaps spending $350 million above and beyond the strategic budget proposed for the next ten years independent of SALT considerations," he says. "Rejection means spending $21 billion more."

The Americans for SALT report said that without the treaty the Soviets could build 750 new strategic nuclear systems, at least 100 more MIRVed ICBM launchers, and put up to 30 or more warheads on each SS-18 missile. "Staying equivalent to the Soviet Union at those escalating levels would require crash programs and expenditures that would dwarf those we would be making under SALT II and would produce less, not more, security than we have today," the report added.

Also without SALT II, treaty-backers said, talks on other important treaties—such as a Comprehensive Test Ban, a ban on satellite and chemical weapons, and the Indian Ocean Arms Limitation Pact, among others—could be suspended indefinitely. They pointed out that failure to ratify SALT II would probably be viewed by nonnuclear nations as evidence that the United States and the Soviet Union were insincere in their obligations, under the Treaty on the Non-Proliferation of Nuclear Weapons, to reduce their own arsenals. Consequently, those nations might see no need to hold back in future procurement of nuclear weapons.

Further, the collapse of SALT II, its proponents said, would increase pressure to scrap the antiballistic missile treaty. If this should happen, it could cost us tens of billions of dollars to build these sophisticated nuclear defense systems.

In summing up many of the arguments of those who favored SALT II, Congressman Aspin admitted that the treaty is far from perfect. Aspin quoted Senator William Proxmire, also of Wisconsin, who has criticized the treaty and has said, "What we need are real reductions in the land-based missiles on both sides."

"He is absolutely correct," agreed Aspin. "However, this is hardly an argument for rejecting SALT II. Let us move on to deeper arms reductions," Aspin said. "Let us agree to start phasing out land-based missiles. Let us propose such things as the banning of any more nuclear weapons production. All of these measures, even in times of minimal political tension, would be most difficult to accomplish. However, if these steps are to be taken at all, SALT II is vital."

12

ON THE DEFENSE AGAIN

Now that SALT II is, for all practical intents and purposes, a dead issue, what happens next? Where do we go from here? Will new negotiations begin, offering more hope for true arms limitations that are fair to all sides? Or will the collapse of SALT II lead to a costly, all-out escalation of the arms race?

Though the answers to these and other pertinent questions are still hidden in the future, it is already apparent that the United States, under the Reagan administration, is now following a policy of security through strength. Greatly disturbed by Soviet gains in military capabilities in recent years, Reagan, Secretary of Defense Casper Weinberger, and other leading administration officials have made the strengthening of the U.S. defense system one of their top priorities.

In a January 1981 news conference, President Reagan said that every Soviet leader since the Russian Revolution, including the present leadership, has repeatedly stated that the Soviet goal is to promote world revolution. "The only morality they recognize is what will further their cause, meaning they reserve unto themselves the right to commit

ROTHCO
The Sacramento Bee

'GETTING HUNGRY IN THERE, BIG FELLA?'

any crime, to lie, to cheat—in order to attain that," Reagan said.

Equally harsh words were voiced at another January 1981 press conference, given by Reagan's secretary of state, General Alexander Haig, former commander of NATO forces. "It's clear that we have been witnessing an unprecedented —at least in character and scope—risk-taking mode on the part of the Soviet Union," Haig said, and added that the Soviets are involved "in conscious policies which foster, support, and expand international terrorism.

"The United States cannot contemplate negotiations or ratifications of arms control agreements exclusive of consideration of the conduct and activities of the Soviet Union outside the sphere of arms control," Haig said. He was referring to aggressive actions the Soviet Union has taken, including the invasion of Afghanistan in December 1979 and threats of retaliation against Polish union workers in 1980 and 1981.

Defense Secretary Weinberger, testifying before the Senate Armed Services Committee, also had sharp words for the Soviet Union: "The Soviet Union has embarked upon a military buildup unprecedented in world history," he said. "The Soviets have relentlessly improved their military capabilities all across the spectrum. The buildup has not been interrupted by détente, the SALT I agreement . . . or the lower level of defense effort on the part of this nation," he said.

What, specifically, did the 1980 Republican party national platform have to say about the issue? Here are some pertinent excerpts:

Despite clear danger signals indicating that Soviet nuclear power would overtake that of the United States by the early 1980s, threatening the survival of the United States, and making possible, for the first time in postwar history, political coercion and defeat, the [Carter] Administration reduced the size and capability of our nuclear forces.

Despite clear danger signals indicating that the Soviet Union was augmenting its military threat to the nations of Western Europe, American defense programs such as the enhanced radiation warhead and cruise missiles, which could have offset that buildup, were canceled or delayed—to the dismay of allies who depend upon American military power for their security.

Mr. Carter [during his administration] canceled production of the Minuteman missile and the B-1 bomber. He delayed all cruise missiles, the MX missile, the Trident submarine and the Trident II missile. He did this while the Soviet Union deployed the Backfire bomber and designed two additional bombers equal in capability to the B-1, and while it deployed four new large ICBMs and developed four others.

Mr. Carter postponed production and deployment of enhanced radiation [neutron] warheads while the Soviet Union deployed the SS-20 mobile missile and the Backfire bomber against Western Europe.

Mr. Carter opposed efforts to correct the terribly inadequate pay rates for our military personnel and stood by as the alarming exodus of trained and skilled personnel from the services quickened. At the same time, the Soviet Union increased its military manpower to a level of 4.8 million, more than double that of the United States.

The Soviet Union is now devoting over $50 billion more to defense annually than the United States, achieving military superiority as a result.

Republicans commit themselves to an immediate increase in defense spending to be applied judiciously to critically needed programs. We will build toward a sustained defense expenditure sufficient to close the gap with the Soviets, and ultimately reach the position of military superiority that the American people demand.

The foreign policy of the United States should reflect a national strategy of peace through strength.

Nuclear weapons are the ultimate military guarantor of American security and that of our allies. Yet since 1977, the United States has moved from essential equivalence to inferiority in strategic nuclear forces with the Soviet Union.

As the disparity between American and Soviet strategic nuclear forces grows over the next three years, most U.S. land-based missiles, heavy bombers, and submarines in port will become vulnerable to a Soviet first-strike. Such a situation invites diplomatic blackmail and a coercion of the United States by the Soviet Union during the coming decade.

Our objective must be to assure the survivability of U.S. forces possessing an unquestioned . . . capability sufficient to disarm Soviet military targets in a second-strike. We reject the mutual-assured-destruction (MAD) strategy of the Carter Administration which limits the President during crises to a choice between mass mutual suicide and surrender. We propose, instead, a credible strategy which will deter a Soviet attack by the clear capability of our forces to survive and ultimately to destroy Soviet military targets.

In order to counter the problem of ICBM vulnerability, we will propose a number of initiatives to provide the necessary survivability of the ICBM force in as timely and effective a manner as possible. In addition, we will proceed with:

- The earliest possible deployment of the MX missile in a prudent survivable configuration.
- Accelerated development and deployment of a new manned strategic bomber. . . .
- Deployment of an air defense system comprised of dedicated modern interceptor aircraft and early-warning support systems.
- Acceleration of development and deployment of strategic cruise missiles. . . .
- Modernization of the military command and control system . . . .

■ 92

■ And vigorous research and development of an effective anti-ballistic missile system . . . as well as more modern ABM technologies.

On the subject of U.S.-Soviet relations, the Republican party platform states: "The premier challenge facing the United States, its allies, and the entire globe is to check the Soviet Union's global ambitions. This challenge must be met, for the present danger is greater than ever before in the 200-year history of the United States. The Soviet Union is still accelerating its drive for military superiority and is intensifying its military pressure and its ideological combat against the industrial democracies and the vulnerable developing nations of the world."

On the general subject of arms reduction negotiations, the platform states: "Republicans believe that the United States can only negotiate with the Soviet Union from a position of unquestioned principle and unquestioned strength.

"As the Soviet Union continues in its expansionist course, the potential for dangerous confrontations has increased. Republicans will strive to resolve critical issues through peaceful negotiations, but we recognize that negotiations conducted from a position of military weakness can result only in further damage to American interests.

"A Republican Administration will continue to seek to negotiate arms reductions. . . . We will pursue hard bargaining for equitable, verifiable, and enforceable agreements. We will accept no agreement for the sake of having an agreement, and will accept no agreements that do not fundamentally enhance our national security.

"We pledge to end the Carter cover-up of Soviet violations of SALT I and II, to end the cover-up of Soviet violation of the Biological Warfare Convention, and to end the cover-up of Soviet use of gas and chemical weapons in Afghanistan and elsewhere."

Fully committed to the party platform on these issues, President Reagan, shortly after taking office, called for an immediate increase in defense spending, while at the same

■ 93

time chopping the federal budget in almost every other area. In October 1981, he announced the development of a "modified" MX system, deploying at least one hundred missiles by the end of the 1980s. But instead of a "mobile" MX system, as former President Carter had proposed, Reagan said that MX missiles would replace older missiles in existing silos, which would be "hardened" to withstand all but a direct hit by Soviet nuclear weapons. Reagan also asked for one hundred new B-1 bombers. Carter had canceled this program, but Reagan said the bombers were needed to replace the aging B-52s. The B-1s, he said, would be used until the Advanced Technology, or "Stealth," bomber could be developed and brought on line in the 1990s. The Stealth is an aircraft that is designed to avoid detection by enemy radar systems.

In addition, in August 1981 President Reagan announced that the United States would proceed with the construction of the neutron bomb. Jimmy Carter had put off making any decision such as this. Defense Secretary Weinberger, early in the Reagan administration, had called for deployment of the neutron bomb in Europe to help bolster NATO forces. "I think that the opportunity that this weapon gives to strengthen tactical nuclear forces is one that we very probably would want to make use of," he said. The neutron bomb, also known as an enhanced radiation weapon, kills people but does not destroy property, and it is designed primarily to offset the Soviet advantage in tank strength. President Reagan in his announcement said that at this time the bomb would not be deployed in Europe but stockpiled here in the United States.

Although Reagan and his aides are clearly stressing a strong military buildup and have rejected SALT II as a viable arms limitation treaty, they nevertheless have left the door open for further negotiations with the Soviet Union.

"I am prepared to discuss a legitimate reduction of nuclear weapons," Reagan said early in 1981. "I have no timetable with regard to discussions that might lead to future negotiations. . . . Any time they [the Soviets] want to sit

"Remember before the neutron bomb
all those silly cartoons about devastation?...."

down and discuss a legitimate reduction of nuclear weapons, I want to go to such negotiations."

It has been less than four decades since the first atomic bomb was tested over the desert near Alamogordo, New Mexico. The awesome destructive power of such a weapon was terrifyingly demonstrated during the latter days of World War II, when bombs were dropped on Japan. Today, nuclear warheads are far more powerful and capable of far greater devastation.

There are, as said earlier, enough nuclear weapons available now to destroy the earth as we know it. The arsenals are well stocked, and the "fuse" could be lit at any time.

But it is not yet a world without hope. The arms race was created by humans. Therefore, it is surely within human capabilities to halt it.

BIBLIOGRAPHY

Books

Caldicott, Helen, M.D. *Nuclear Madness: What You Can Do!* Brookline, Mass.: Authum Press, 1978.

Falwell, Jerry. *Listen America.* New York: Doubleday & Co., Inc., 1980.

Myrdal, Alva. *The Game of Disarmament.* New York: Pantheon Books, 1977.

Thompson, Carol L., "Cold War" in *The World Book Encyclopedia*, Vol. 4, pp. 618–618i. Chicago: World Book–Childcraft International, Inc., 1978.

Booklets, Pamphlets, Documents, and Bulletins

Americans for SALT. *Salt Talk.* Vol. 1, Nos. 2 and 5.

Americans for SALT. *News Bulletin,* April 19, 1979.

Coalition for Peace through Strength. *An Analysis of SALT II.* Second ed. Washington, D.C.: 1979.

The United Nations Disarmament Yearbook. Vol. 3, 1978.

United Nations. *Disarmament: A Periodic Review.* Vol. II, Nos. 1 (May 1979) and 2 (October 1979).

United States, Arms Control and Disarmament Agency. *The Dangers of Nuclear Proliferation.*

United States, Arms Control and Disarmament Agency. *19th Annual Report* (1979).

United States, Congress. *Congressional Record.* March 1, 1977; July 1, 1979; July 24, 1979; October 27, 1979.

United States, Congress, Senate, Armed Services Committee. *The Military Implications of the Proposed SALT II Treaty.* Report, December 20, 1979.

United States, Congress, Senate, Committee on Foreign Relations. *The SALT II Treaty.* Report, November 1979.

United States, Department of Defense. *Annual Report.* 1981.

United States, Department of State. *Compliance with SALT I Agreements; Verification of SALT II Agreement*, July 1979; August 1979.

United States, Department of State. *SALT II Agreement, Vienna, June 18, 1979.* Selected Documents Series, 12A and 12B.

United States, Department of State. *SALT II and American Security.* Publication No. 0-281-552(543). Washington, D.C.: Government Printing Office, June 1979.

United States, Department of State. *SALT II: The Path of Security and Peace.* Current Policy Bulletin No. 66, April 1979.

United States, Department of State. *SALT II: The Reasons Why.* Publication 8978.

United States, Department of State. *SALT II: Two Views.* Current Policy Bulletin No. 66, April 1979.

United States, Department of State. *The Strategic Arms Limitation Talks.* Special Report No. 46, May 1979.

United States, Government Printing Office. *U.S. Military Posture for 1980.* Publication No. 623-708/848, 1979.

United States, Library of Congress, Congressional Research Staff. *Defense Budget 1981.* Issue Brief 80037.

United States, Senate Foreign Relations Committee. *SALT II: Senate Testimony, July 9–11, 1979.*

INDEX

■ 99